How To Keep Your Faith While In College

Dr. Robert Morey

WORLD
BIBLE PUBLISHERS, INC.
Iowa Falls, IA 50126 U.S.A.

Unless otherwise noted, all Scripture quotations are either the author's own or from the New American Standard Bible, copyrighted The Lockman Foundation 1960, 1962, 1963, 1968, 1971, 1972, 1973, 1975, 1977, and are by permission.

World Bible Publishers, Inc.
Iowa Falls, IA 50126

Printed in the United States of America

ISBN 0-529-11368-6

1 2 3 4 5 BGP 05 04 03 02 01

About the Author

Dr. Bob Morey, Executive Director of the Research and Education Foundation, is the author of over forty books, some of which have been translated into French, German, Italian, Polish, Finnish, Dutch, Spanish, Norwegian, Swedish, and Chinese. He has doctorates in apologetics and Islamic studies. For more information on his ministry, write to:

Faith Defenders
P.O. Box 7447
Orange, CA 92863

www.faithdefenders.com
1-800-41-TRUTH

Other books by Dr. Morey:

Fearing God
The Trinity: Evidence and Issues
Satan's Devices
The Islamic Invasion
The Truth about Masons
Death and the Afterlife

Dedication

Dedicated to
John and Ruthanne

Table of Contents

Introduction

One of the most important abilities a student must have as he attends college or university is DISCERNMENT. Discernment is the ability to distinguish, discriminate and judge between what is true and what is not true, what is good and what is evil.

In the Scriptures, discernment is referred to in such places as Gen. 31:32, where we are told to discern the difference between what belongs to us and what belongs to others. We are also to discern good from evil (II Sam. 14:15; 19·35; I Kgs. 3:9; Heb. 5:14), justice from injustice (I Kgs. 3:11), the holy from the profane, the clean from the unclean (Ezk. 44:23), the righteous from the wicked (Mal. 3:18) and those who serve God and those who do not serve God (Mal. 3:18).

Discernment also means understanding the times in which we live. This was the praise accorded to the men of Issachar "who understood the times and knew what Israel should do" (I Chron. 12:32). Discernment is the opposite of "gullibility." Gullibility is the naive and childish acceptance of whatever the professor or textbook teaches. It is the foolish assumption that if something were not true it would not be printed in a book. Or, if it were not true, the professor would not teach it.

In order to be discerning, we must understand the truth (I Kgs. 3:9, 11-14; Pro. 2:2). In order to have understanding, we need God's wisdom (Pro. 10:23). And, in order to have wisdom, we must learn to fear the God who made us (Pro.

1:7, 16:6; II Tim. 2:7).

This means that no Christian student should be so gullible as to simply accept whatever the professor says or what the textbook teaches. It does not matter if he is on a Christian or secular campus. He must learn to discern the world view that is being taught by the professor or textbook. This is what the Bible recommends in such places as Acts 17:11.

Some students lose their faith while at a Christian college because their professors taught them a humanistic world view. Having spoken at many Christian colleges, it is obvious that much of what is called "Christian" education is nothing more than secular humanism sprinkled with a few religious terms. Just because the professor begins his class with prayer does not automatically mean that he is going to teach the Christian world and life view. A student must be discerning regardless of what college he attends.

Judge Not Lest Ye Be Judged

One of the rationalizations which some people use to escape their biblical responsibility to judge between truth and error is the popular saying, "Judge not lest ye be judged." The vague meaning that is sometimes given to this statement is that we should not judge anyone about anything. Thus when we judge that abortion is murder, the abortionists respond, "Judge not." When we judge that a certain professor is teaching humanism, he cries out, "Judge not." When we judge that unwed mothers are guilty of the sin of fornication, people cry out, "Judge not." We are told that we should never say anything negative about anyone, no matter what they have done.

The problem with a non-judgmental view of life is that it contradicts Scripture. When Jesus said not to judge in Matt. 7:1, He was not speaking to His disciples. He was speaking to the hypocrites who would condemn someone for doing something they themselves were doing (v. 5)! In other words, you don't have the moral right to stand up and condemn other people for being immoral if you are immoral yourself! Jesus was condemning hypocritical judgments.

On the other hand, Jesus commanded His disciples to judge people as false prophets (Matt. 7:6-20) He told them to "judge a righteous judgement" in John 7:24. He Himself had no problem judging people (Matt. 23:13-39).

A non-judgmental view of life is also absurd. If we did not judge whether people were saved or not, no one could be baptized or join the church. There could be no church discipline if we did not judge people. No criminals would be tried or convicted. Lazy people could not be fired if we could not judge them as lazy. Sick people could not be treated unless we judged them sick. In short, human society would be destroyed if everyone was non-judgmental.

The Apostle Paul repeatedly warned us not to let people deceive us (I Cor. 6:9-11; Gal. 5:19-21). If they are pagans, we should judge them so. If they claim to be Christians but disobey God's law, John tells us to judge them as liars (I John 2:4).

The loving thing to do is to judge people according to Scriptural standards. Yes, there will be opposition if you judge righteous judgments. Did not people oppose Jesus? But this opposition is hypocritical because they are judging you for judging! They are condemning you for condemning others! If they really believe that judging others is wrong, then how can they turn around and judge you? So, don't be intimidated by them. Boldly point out their hypocrisy. You have God's Word on your side (Rom. 8:31).

As you study this survival manual, you will be challenged and forced to think deeply about the ultimate questions of life. We will be as frank and as bold as the authors of Scriptures and the Lord Jesus Himself. Never be afraid of the truth. It can only bring you closer to the God who is the Origin of all truth.

ONE

Taking the First Steps

As you prepare to enter college, you need to think about WHY you are going to college. If you do not have clear goals which designate exactly what you want to accomplish at college, you will experience frustration and will end up wasting a lot of time and money. Remember,

> "If you aim at nothing,
> you are bound to hit it.
> If you fail to plan,
> you plan to fail."

In the New Testament, we are told that we are to run the race that God has set before us (Heb. 12:1-2). And we should not think that it is enough just to make it to the end. We must run to *win!* We must strive for excellence in all that we do. This is how the Apostle Paul put it,

> "Do you not know that in a race all the runners run, but only one gets the prize? Run in such a way as to get the prize. Everyone who competes in the games goes into strict training. They do it to get a crown that will not last; but we do it to get a crown that will last forever. Therefore I do not run like a man running aimlessly; I do not fight like a man beating the air."
>
> (I Cor. 9:24-26)

The Curse of Mediocrity

Since the Scriptures call us to strive to do the best we can in whatever we do, we must not fall into the curse of mediocrity. The curse of mediocrity would have us believe that the most important thing in life is to be a "balanced" person. Thus we should not work too hard at anything. We should do only what is required of us. We should not attempt to excel or to be superior in anything that we do. The absolute minimum should be the highest we go. In other words, we should only be "one of the guys," i.e., an "average" or "balanced" person.

The Chief End of Man

Mediocrity is condemned by such Scriptures as I Cor. 10:31 and Col. 3:23 where we are told that man exists to glorify God. Thus the glory of God is the goal of man's existence. We must excel to do the very best we can unto the glory of our Creator who is the Sovereign Lord of the universe.

Do you live unto the glory of God? The Apostle Paul said that whenever we do anything we should do it to God's glory. Thus we cannot be lazy, sloppy, or mediocre. We must strive to *do* the very best we can in order to *be* the best we can for the glory of God. Pause right now and say to yourself, "I exist for the glory of God."

This perspective is desperately needed today because far too many people think that God exists to make people happy. They view God as some kind of heavenly vending machine that exists for the pleasure of man. They demand that God provide them with whatever they want and then they get bitter if they do not get it. But God does not exist for man's happiness. Man exists for the glory of God.

The glory of God thus becomes the main motivation for excellence in academic studies. We do not want to bring shame on the name or cause of Christ by being sloppy or shoddy in our academic work. We want to bring glory to Christ and His Gospel. As Jesus taught us in Matt. 5:16,

"Let your light shine before men, that they may see your good deeds and glorify your Father in heaven."

The Apostle Paul also commands us in I Cor. 10:31,

"So whether you eat or drink or whatever you do, do it all for the glory of God."

Living for the glory of God means that instead of striving to do the absolute minimum to get by, we must strive to do the maximum to be the best that we can to the glory of God. If we have a class assignment that asks for a ten page paper, we will try to do fifteen pages. If we have a reading assignment of two books, we will read three or more books. Our motto will be, "Only the best for God." In other words, you have to *work* to glorify God. God is never glorified by laziness.

Diligence vs. Slothfulness

The book of Proverbs constantly tells us that diligence and hard work are the keys to success. Laziness leads to poverty and failure.

"Lazy hands make a man poor, but diligent hands bring wealth."

(Pro. 10:4)

"Diligent hands will rule, but laziness ends in slave labor."

(Pro. 12:24)

"Do you see a man skilled in his work? He will serve before kings; he will not serve before obscure men."

(Pro. 22:29)

We must be diligent and hard working in all that we do. This means that we should not be lazy or slothful. We should excel to do the most and to be the best of which we are capable. Thus instead of viewing college as "party time," we should view college as a time for glorifying God. Instead of wasting time, we should be preparing to be successful in life.

Make no doubt about it. Academic success now will reap financial rewards in the future. Be not deceived on this point. If you are lazy and slothful while in college, you will probably be lazy and slothful when you get out of college. Proverbs tells us that only the diligent and hardworking will be rewarded by the fruits of their labor.

Losing Your Soul

Many students began their college experience with their Christian faith intact. But by the time of their senior year, many of them no longer attend church or even claim to be "saved." What happened to their commitment to Christ?

The vast majority of students lose their faith because they fall prey to the temptations of immorality and drugs. In the vast majority of cases there were no lofty ideals or motives behind their apostasy. Neither were there any great intellectual problems which caused them to abandon the Church. They left the faith because it stood in the way of their own personal pleasure.

In Jesus' "Parable of the Sower," only one out of the four professing Christians was really saved. The other three fell away because of a lack of interest, peer pressure, persecution, trials and the temptations of this world (see: Matt. 13:1-9).

The Warnings of Scripture

Because so many students lose their faith during their college experience, we would do well to pause and consider the causes of their apostasy. The Scriptures warn us in many places that there is the ever present danger of departing from the faith.

"Be self-controlled and alert. Your enemy the devil prowls around like a roaring lion looking for someone to devour."

(I Pet. 5:8)

"Turn away from godless chatter and the opposing ideas of what is falsely called knowledge, which some have professed and in so doing have wandered from the faith."

(I Tim. 6:20, 21)

"See to it that no one takes you captive through hollow and deceptive philosophy, which depends on human tradition and the basic principles of this world rather than on Christ."

(Col. 2:8)

While the Scriptures repeatedly warn us that it is possible for someone who *professes* to be saved to fall away from the faith (Heb. 6:4-6), this is in contrast to someone who actually *possesses* true salvation. The Apostle John tells us that a true believer cannot fall away.

"They went out from us, but they did not really belong to us. For if they had belonged to us, they would have remained with us; but their going showed that none of them belonged to us."

(I John 2:19)

Are You Real or Counterfeit?

It is very important that you make sure that you are a *real* Christian and not a counterfeit because there are many people today who think they are saved when in reality they have never personally known God. Jesus warned us of this possibility in Matt. 7:21-23.

Many people believe in Christ because they were raised in

a Christian home and attended a Christian church. They "prayed" to "receive" Jesus and have run down countless aisles at church or camp meetings. Perhaps they were leaders in their youth group. But regardless of their experience in the church, once they got to college they soon abandoned their faith.

What should your attitude be as you enter college? Should you smugly assume that you are saved and that all is well? What did the Apostle Paul say in I Cor. 10:12?

"So, if you think you are standing firm, be careful that you don't fall!"

If we take the Bible seriously, then we must examine ourselves to see if we are really in the faith.

"Examine yourselves to see whether you are in the faith; test yourselves."

(II Cor. 13:5)

"Therefore, my brothers, be all the more eager to make your calling and election sure. For if you do these things, you will never fall."

(II Pet. 1:10)

In the light of these Scriptures, it is clear that the most important priority in your life as you prepare to go to college is to make sure that you truly know the Lord Jesus Christ as your personal Lord and Savior.

How to Know If You Are Really Saved

In order for you to discern if you have had a true conversion experience, it is necessary to think through some of the biblical evidences and tests of regeneration. The entire book of First John is the fullest treatment of the assurance of salvation in the New Testament.

In I John 5:13 we are told,

"I write these things to you who believe in the name of the Son of God so that you may know that you have eternal life."

Just as John gave us the theme for his entire Gospel in John 20:31, he also gave us the theme for his entire Epistle of I John in 5:13. Since John is dealing with the subject of how we can know if we are really saved, he lays out his material in a very logical and orderly manner.

An important distinction must be pointed out at this juncture. Salvation and assurance of salvation are NOT the same thing. Salvation has to do with justification which is by faith alone in Christ by grace alone. This is in contrast to assurance of salvation which has to do with sanctification, i.e., the Christian life.

Salvation deals with the issue of "being" while assurance deals with "well-being." Salvation determines whether you get to heaven while assurance determines how happy you are along the way. While obedience and works do not play a role in salvation, they do play a vital role in assurance of salvation. Your life must back up your lip when it comes to assurance of salvation.

Throughout the New Testament we are told that the proof of true salvation is obedience (John 8:12, 31; 14:15, 21-23; 15:14; I Cor. 6:9-11; II Cor. 5:17; Gal. 5:19-23). We do not have the right to say that we are saved if we are living in disobedience at the same time (I John 2:4). While the grounds of our salvation is grace alone, the test of our assurance of salvation is obedience.

In his Epistle, the Apostle John constantly challenges our assurance by saying, "Hereby we know Him if. . . . " He demands that we "prove" or "test" our assurance of salvation. This proof is obtained by self-examination. John calls upon us to examine our lives to see if God has truly given us a new heart.

I. Examine Your Faith

The first thing that John calls us to examine is our faith. John stresses that there are two distinct areas of faith which we must examine in order to see if we are truly the children of God.

A. The Content of Your Faith

First John tells us to examine the content of our faith. This means that what we believe about God, the Bible, Jesus Christ, salvation, sin, etc., is very important. If we do not believe in the historic Christian Faith, then we are not saved.

> "This is how you can recognize the Spirit of God: Every spirit that acknowledges that Jesus Christ has come in the flesh is from God."
>
> (I John 4:2)

> "If anyone acknowledges that Jesus is the Son of God, God lives in him and he in God."
>
> (I John 4:15)

> "Everyone who believes that Jesus is the Christ is born of God."
>
> (I John 5:1)

As you enter college, you will meet people who openly deny that Jesus was the Christ. Marxist and atheistic professors will even claim that Jesus never existed and thus Jesus is a myth! Other people will claim that Jesus was only a humble Jewish rabbi, a moral teacher or a good example. Occultists will claim that all men are little christs and gods!

The issue of whether Jesus was *the* Christ is so important that the Apostle John said that anyone who denied it was a liar and an antichrist!

> "Who is the liar? It is the man who denies that Jesus is the Christ. Such a man is the antichrist — he denies

the Father and the Son. No one who denies the Son
has the Father; whoever acknowledges the Son has the
Father also.''

(I John 2:22, 23)

John warned us not to accept false prophets and their false
doctrines. We must test all religious claims and teachings according to Scripture.

"Dear friends, do not believe every spirit, but test the
spirits to see whether they are from God, because many
false prophets have gone out into the world . . . every
spirit that does not acknowledge Jesus is not from God.
This is the spirit of the antichrist, which you have heard
is coming and even now is already in the world."

(I John 4:1-3)

Sincerity Is Not Enough!

Do not be fooled by the rather stupid idea that it does not
really matter what you believe as long as you are sincere. The
Apostle John makes it absolutely clear that if someone does
not believe in the Gospel, they are already under the just condemnation of God (John 3:18).

What can you say to people who are so foolish to think
that sincerity is enough in religion? Point out to them that since
sincerity is never enough anywhere else in life, why should it
be enough in religion? Is sincerity enough in medicine, law,
finances or politics? Ask them,

Do you really believe that it does not matter what a
doctor does as long as he is sincere?
How a lawyer handles a case as long as he is sincere?
How a financial manager handles money as long as he
is sincere?
What a politician does as long as he is sincere?
If you got on a bus sincerely thinking you were on your

way to New York City, when you actually got on
a bus going to California, would your sincerity alter
the fact that you are going in the wrong direction?
Sincerity has nothing to do with the issue of Truth.
Can't we be sincerely wrong?

Logic and Religion

Logically speaking, since all religions contradict each other,
either one religion is the true religion or none of them are true.
They cannot all be true. But what do we say if we run across
someone who says,

"I have my truth and you have your truth. Truth is
whatever you want it to be."

Point out to them that they are hypocrites because they
do not really believe such nonsense. They cannot live what they
believe. For example, if their bank took away all their money
and said, "We have our truth that you never gave us any
money, and you have your truth that you did," this person
would be the first to say that we must be objective and rational!

The Parent Trap

Another possible snare you must avoid at all costs is the
blind faith of some parents. Now it is clear that Christian parents should desire that their children come to know and love
the Lord Jesus early in life. This desire is one evidence that
they are saved. A parent who claims to be saved but does not
manifest any concern to see his children saved is no more saved
than a stone.

While the desire to see your children saved is proper and
necessary, some parents become so desperate to believe that
their children are saved that they will grasp at anything. Even
when their son or daughter openly denies the faith and en-

gages in gross wickedness, they will still comfort themselves by saying,

> "Well, at least my son is saved. He may not act like it now but I know he is saved because he accepted Jesus when he was five years old. He doesn't go to church anymore and married a Catholic but I still say he is saved."

Instead of facing the reality that their child is on his way to hell, some parents will cling to false hopes so they can sleep at night. But instead of seeking their own psychological comfort, they should seek the conversion of their child by telling him the truth. Many sons and daughters have ended up in hell because their parents repeatedly told them that they were saved even while they were living in wickedness. Instead of helping their children, they damned them forever.

Salvation Is a Work of God

The basic problem is that we tend to forget that salvation is a work of God and not a work of man. We are not saved because we prayed but because *God* gave us a new heart. In such places as John 1:13; 3:3, 5 and Rom. 9:16, we are repeatedly told that God saves us by His power and not by our prayers.

Some people have a magical view of prayer in which if anyone, regardless of his age or understanding, prays certain words such as "Come into my heart, Lord Jesus," he is automatically saved! It never dawns on them that salvation is something the Lord does. Salvation is not worked by such magical incantations.

God is viewed as a vending machine that mechanically dispenses salvation the moment someone pushes the right button by saying the right words. Thus they get their children to ask Jesus into their heart and then they sit back and comfort themselves that their children are saved regardless if there is ever any evidence that God has truly done a work in their hearts.

The only way that we can know if God has saved our children is by their lifestyle. If they are saved, they have become new creatures in Christ and will show it by a change in their attitudes and actions (II Cor. 5:17). In other words, there will be clear evidence in their lives that God has worked true repentance and faith in their hearts. Thus they will:

1. Thirst after the living God (Psa. 42:2).
2. Hunger after righteousness (Matt. 5:6).
3. Talk about the Lord and seek Christian fellowship (Mal. 3:16-18).
4. Be fervent in prayer (Gal. 4:6).
5. Be interested in, read, and enjoy Scripture (Psa. 1; 119:9, 11).
6. Love the Law of God (Psa. 119:97).
7. Go to church because they want to (Psa. 84).

If you are truly saved, you will show it by the way you live.

B. The Character of Your Faith

John not only tells us to examine the content of our faith but also the character or kind of faith we have. This is why in the Greek, John always uses the word "believe" in the present tense. He never refers to a date or a decision in the past as the basis of one's assurance of salvation.

Not once in the New Testament does anyone claim to be saved because they "made a decision" in the past. Rather we are told that assurance of salvation is always based on the present fact of personal trust in the Lord Jesus Christ.

"Everyone who [is believing right now] that Jesus is the Christ is born of God."

(I John 5:1)

In John 3:16, John refers to faith in the present tense.

"For God so loved the world that He gave His only begotten Son, that whosoever [is believing right now] in him shall not perish but have eternal life."

When people apply for membership in a church, if the only question they are asked is "When were you saved?" a terrible mistake has been made. Where was such a question ever asked in Scripture? Far too many people base their assurance of salvation solely on some decision they made in the past when there is nothing presently in their lives to show that they love God!

Far too many churches are filled with unregenerate people whose unspiritual lives are excused by calling them "carnal Christians" or "nominal Christians." They only show up Sunday morning. They never volunteer for anything. They are not interested in studying the Bible. They don't witness at work or have private or family devotions. They are more concerned about the building than the ministry. They are pragmatists who consistently ignore or disobey Scripture. In short, there is no evidence in their lives that they are really saved. Their "assurance" of salvation is based solely on some event in the past which has no bearing on the present. Such professions of faith are quite worthless, says James (James 2:14-26). While works do not save us, once we are saved, we will work for the Lord (Eph. 2:8-10). When someone wants to join a church, they should be asked,

"What evidence do you see in your life right now that would lead you to believe that God has given you a new heart?"

This kind of question will reveal false confessions of faith and lead to true conversions. It will focus on the present spiritual state of people and deal with their present situation.

Questions to Ask Yourself

As you prepare to leave high school, ask yourself:

Am I really a Christian?
Have I really been saved?
Do I truly love and serve the Lord Jesus Christ?
Do I have a personal relationship with Him?
Do I live to bring glory to God?
What evidence is there in my life that proves that I am
    saved?

Is it not better to search your soul *now* before you get to college, than to be overwhelmed by temptations once you get there? Many young people, like Judas, thought they were Christians. But in the end, it was revealed that they had never truly been saved. You must search your soul to make sure that you know the Lord Jesus Christ as your own personal Savior. If you have never made that step of commitment on your own then you should do so now.

One of the reasons why we must examine ourselves to see if we are really saved is that childhood conversions seldom work out. Indeed, most of the young people who stop attending church after they reach the age of 18 had a childhood conversion in which they prayed to "receive" Jesus. But their conversion was psychological instead of spiritual.

The sad truth is that the vast majority of childhood conversions never pan out. Most churches experience a 75% or greater drop out rate for their young people. While it is true that God can save a child, it is also true that we can get a child to pray to "receive" Bozo the Clown or Jesus with equal success. Beware of false assurance.

II. Examine Your Life

The Apostle John tells us to examine the way we live. He calls us to examine our lives in two ways.

A. Examine Your Heart: Your Attitudes

One of the clearest evidences of true conversion is a proper attitude toward God's Law. In I John 5:3 we are told that God's commandments are not grievous or burdensome. This means that the true child of God does not view God's Law as a straightjacket which keeps him from true happiness. Instead, a real Christian will view God's Law as containing the principles of success and true happiness in life.

> "Do not let this Book of the Law depart from your mouth; meditate on it day and night, so that you may be careful to do everything written in it. Then you will be prosperous and successful."
>
> (Joshua 1:8)

In order to examine your own heart to see if you are truly saved, ask yourself the following questions:

Do I love the Law of God or do I view it as something that is keeping me from true happiness?

Do I prize God's Law as principles of success or as a club to beat me down?

Do I view the Law as a hindrance to what I really want to do?

One of the clearest evidences of salvation is when someone comes to *love* the Law of God with all of his heart. In Psalm 119:97, David reveals the child of God *loves* the Law of the Lord. When someone is saved, God writes His Law in his heart (Jer. 31:33-34) and he will never depart from Him (Jer. 32:40). If your attitude toward the Law of God is negative then you must question whether or not God has ever given you a new heart.

The Apostle John not only tells us to examine our attitude to the Law of God, but he also calls upon us to examine the emotional focus of our lives (I John 2:9-11, 15-17).

Do we love what God loves and hate what God hates? If we love what God hates then we are the enemies of God (James

4:4). If we hate what God loves then we are not on God's side. We are to think God's thoughts after Him and to love what God loves and hate what God hates.

If someone is truly converted, he will love the people of God and seek out and enjoy Christian fellowship. He will love to talk about the Lord with those who know Him. This is how the righteous can be distinguished from the wicked according to Mal. 3:16-18. John also teaches this truth in the N.T.

> "We know that we have passed from death to life, because we love our brothers."
>
> (I John 3:14)

> "Dear friends, let us love one another, for love comes from God. Everyone who loves has been born of God and knows God."
>
> (I John 4:7)

On the other hand, if we hate what God loves and love the things of this world instead, then we know that the love of the Father is not in us.

> "Do not love the world or anything in the world. If anyone loves the world, the love of the Father is not in him. For everything in the world — the cravings of sinful man, the lust of his eyes and the boasting of what he has and does — comes not from the Father but from the world."
>
> (I John 2:15, 16)

This means that we must ask ourselves some questions.

Do I naturally gravitate toward other Christians or do I naturally hang out with non-Christians?
Do I seek out the company of "spiritual" Christians or do I seek the company of "carnal" Christians?

It is a wise saying that, "Birds of a feather flock together." This means that who you choose to be your friends will indicate the true spiritual state of your heart. If you seek the company of non-Christians who are worldly in mind, attitude and actions, then you are probably not saved no matter how many times you have "prayed" or run down an aisle. The Apostle Paul warned us in I Cor. 15:33,

> "Be not deceived, evil company will corrupt good behavior."

During your high school experience, did you seek the company of those who loved the Lord or did you run with the non-Christian crowd? If you naturally gravitated to the company of non-Christians, you did so because you felt more comfortable around them. This is a good indication that you are not saved.

B. Examine Your Life: Your Actions

Those who claim to love and know Christ and yet willfully disregard and disobey His Law do not give any evidence of true conversion.

> "The man who says, 'I know him,' but does not do what he commands is a liar, and the truth is not in him."
>
> (I John 2:4)

Jesus explicitly taught that obedience to God's Law is the clearest evidence of true conversion.

> "If you love me, you will keep my commandments."
>
> (John 14:23)

> "If you abide in my word, then you are truly my disciples."
>
> (John 8:31)

The kind of obedience demanded in Scripture is *purposeful* obedience, not perfect obedience. While a true Christian sins in many ways every day (James 3:2), yet he continues daily to purpose in his heart not to sin against God's Law. Sin aggravates him and disturbs him. It is an unwelcomed guest.

He yearns for holiness more than happiness.

The Apostle John was very wise in calling upon us to examine ourselves to see if we are truly saved. What if we were to gain the whole world but lose our immortal soul? Of what profit would there be if we deceive ourselves into thinking that we are saved when we are not saved?

Do not be deceived. The truth is never afraid of examination. The light is never afraid of exposure. If you are saved, all the self-examination in the world will not unsave you. If you are truly converted, you will not lose your salvation because you question it. Doubts have never damned anyone but false confidence has led millions into hell. If you are not converted and you do not examine yourself then you will go on thinking you are saved when in reality you are still under the wrath of Almighty God.

What If You Fail the Test?

What if you have come to the conclusion that you do not have the evidences of true conversion as given by the Apostle John?

First of all, face reality. Don't try to evade or ignore the fact that your life does not have the evidences required by Scripture as manifesting true conversion. Don't try to run from the problem or cover it over with cheap shoddy prayers or quick decisions. Don't run down the nearest aisle and make some emotional demonstration in the attempt to delude yourself into yet another false conversion.

Second, tell your pastor that you doubt your salvation and that you want the real thing this time. Ask him to pray for you as you seek the Lord by yourself for the first time in your life.

It is important that you seek the Lord all by yourself because when you get to college your pastor and your parents will not be there to help you. You will have to stand up on your own two feet. You must know within yourself where you stand with God.

This perhaps is the most important turning point in your life. Jeremiah 29:13 says that if you seek the Lord with all of your heart you will certainly find him. In Rom. 10:13, the Apostle Paul says,

> "Whoever shall call upon the name of the Lord shall be saved."

These precious promises point you toward the Lord Jesus Christ as the only one who can save you.

Perhaps the following prayer will help you in your commitment to Christ. Such a commitment could well be the turning point in your life as you prepare to enter college. The words are not magical. This is just an example of how to cry out to the Lord for salvation.

> "Lord Jesus, I confess to you and all of heaven that I am a sinner and that I cannot save myself. You have done everything that is needed for my salvation. I ask you to give me a new heart. Work salvation in me. Save me as I now submit to your Lordship over all of my life. Please make me your servant."

The issue of assurance of salvation involves submission to the Lordship of Christ. Don't be deceived by those who peddle a cheap assurance in which you can have Jesus as Savior without bowing to Him as Lord (Rom. 10:9; Col. 2:6). You cannot cut the Lord Jesus Christ into pieces and accept only a part of Him.

After one is saved, the Lordship of Christ over all of life must be reaffirmed *daily*. This is why the Apostle Peter when writing to fellow Christians reminded them to renew Christ's Lordship in their hearts.

> "In your hearts set apart Christ as Lord."
>
> (I Pet. 3:15)

The Lordship of Christ means that you are willing to live for the glory of God and to demonstrate that God's will for your life is perfect, good and acceptable. Thus in Rom. 12:1, 2, the Apostle Paul tells us to present ourselves as a living sacrifice to God.

> "Therefore, I urge you, brothers, in view of God's mercy, to offer your bodies as living sacrifices, holy and pleasing to God — which is your spiritual worship. Do not conform any longer to the pattern of this world, but be transformed by the renewing of your mind. Then you will be able to test and approve what God's will is — his good, pleasing and perfect will."

Have you made a definite commitment to serve God all the days of your life? Have you surrendered everything in your life to the Lordship of Christ? Have you made Christ the Lord of your life? Do you seek to serve Him in all you do? Do you seek His will for your life or do you seek to do only what you want?

The Lordship of Christ is not something that we once affirmed and then never bother with again. It is not to be viewed as some cheap decision that we made at an altar years ago. Since we face temptations to sin and to unbelief daily, we must reaffirm our commitment to the Lordship of Christ daily. This is why the Lord Jesus Christ emphasized that we must take up our cross and deny ourselves daily.

> "If anyone would come after me, he must deny himself and take up his cross daily and follow me."
>
> (Luke 9:23-26)

Perhaps the following prayer will help you to reaffirm the Lordship of Christ in your life. This is not meant to be a once and for all experience or commitment to Christ. Neither should you view these words as magical. Merely saying these words will not do anything. But it is the God to whom you pray who may can work true repentance and submission in your heart. This prayer is intended to be an example of the daily affirmation of the Lordship of Christ that should take place in the life of every true believer.

"Lord Jesus, I love you because you first loved me. Just as you gave your life for me, I now give my life to you. I present my body as a living sacrifice to you that I may prove that your will is good and acceptable. I now reaffirm your Lordship over all of life."

Summary

The Bible calls upon Christians to bow before the Lordship of Christ. We cannot say, "Come in Savior but stay out Lord." We must put our trust and confidence in the Lord Jesus Christ for if the foundation be false, the house cannot stand. The first step toward Christian maturity is to discern where you stand in your relationship with God.

Questions for Discussion

1. What are my goals in life?
2. What role does God play in the decisions I make and the goals I set? What conclusion must be drawn if God does not really make a difference in my life?
3. Do I live for the glory of God or only for my own personal pleasure?
4. What evidence is there in my life that God has given me a new heart?
5. Do I hunger and thirst after righteousness or only after the things of this world?
6. Do I feel more comfortable among non-Christians or among Christians?
7. Do I desire to serve the Lord to the best of my ability or do I think only of personal pleasure, affluence, and popularity?
8. Do I view God, the Bible, the Church, and God's Law as hindrances or helps in my life?

9. Do I strive for excellence and success or do I settle for being mediocre?

10. Do I want to find, follow and finish God's will for my life or do I want to fulfill my own goals in life?

T W O

Knowing the God Who Made You

Have you ever asked yourself the question, "Why am I here?" One of the marks of maturity is that we begin to ask ourselves the ultimate questions of life. Have you ever wondered where you came from, why you are here, and where you are going? These questions focus on issues which are essential to an understanding of human existence. If you cannot answer them or your answer is wrong, you will not be able to live life to its fullest.

The secular humanists of the 20th Century ignore the great questions of life because they have finally come to the conclusion that there are no *secular* answers to such questions. They are quite aware of the *religious* answers which center in God as the Origin of Meaning. But they refuse to consider religion as a viable answer. Thus they do not want people to ask themselves questions concerning the origin, nature, purpose, or destiny of human life. Such questions invariably lead to God.

By coming to the conclusion that life is without meaning, the humanists have completely verified what Solomon wrote in the book of Ecclesiastes thousands of years ago. In this book, Solomon points out that if one begins without God, life will have no meaning. Regardless if one considers wealth, knowledge, power, or respect among men, life without God is nothing but "vanity of vanities."

The book of Proverbs, in contrast to Ecclesiastes, teaches

us that if one begins with God, life will have meaning and significance. The key to a fulfilling life of meaning, significance and dignity is the knowledge of God (Pro. 1:7).

Man was created to know and enjoy his Creator. This is why the Westminster Catechism states as its first point of teaching that the "end" or the purpose of man is "to glorify God and to enjoy Him forever."

Christians believe in a God-centered universe. In other words, the universe exists for the glory and pleasure of God (Rev. 4:11). This includes mankind. Thus we exist in order to bring glory to our Creator.

This is in stark opposition to a humanistic view of life in which man is the center of the universe. If a god or gods are allowed to exist, they exist only to serve man. Thus the happiness of man becomes the goal of life instead of the glory of God.

The Bible opens with the words, "In the beginning God," because God must always come first in all things. Thus the infinite God of Scripture is the Origin, Judge, and Basis of truth, justice, morals, meaning and beauty. If you begin with God you can have these things but if you begin with man you will end in chaos and confusion in which there is no truth.

The history of philosophy eloquently demonstrates that whenever we attempt to view man as the measure of all things, we always end up with skepticism and relativism. Because man is finite and sinful, he is not sufficient in and of himself to be the origin or judge of truth. Only the infinite God of Scripture can serve as the Origin of all things.

With this understanding, the knowledge of God becomes the chief purpose of life. Indeed, the apostle Paul tells us that he viewed everything else in life as nothing more than garbage when compared to the excellency of the knowledge of Christ (Phil. 3:8-10). In John 17:3, Jesus said that the knowledge of God is the central meaning of the eternal life offered to us in the Gospel.

If you are a real Christian, the smile and the frown of God is the most important thing in life. Because you know and love

God, you will try to avoid those things which offend Him. You will seek to please Him in all that you do (II Cor. 5:9). You will no longer live unto yourself but unto Him who died and rose for you (II Cor. 5:15).

The knowledge of God not only concerns the heart but also the mind. Thus the Scriptures not only urge us to submit ourselves to God as His servants, but also to understand the nature and character of the God who made us. The first commandment found in the Decalogue has to do with obtaining a true and accurate understanding of the nature of God (Exo. 20:3).

False views of God lead to false views of the universe and man himself. Since we must begin with God, we must begin with a true and accurate understanding of the God who made us.

Theism comes in two forms: monotheism and polytheism.

Monotheism

Monotheism is the belief that there is only one God who exists apart from and independently of the existence of the material universe. God thus does not depend upon the approval or the belief of man for His existence. God is not the creation or projection of man's hopes or fears. His existence does not rely upon man's wishes or prayers. God truly exists in His own being or essence as a cognitive ego who says, "I am that I am."

In this sense, God is the supreme Being who manifests the attributes of personhood. God thinks, plans, chooses and acts independent of the existence of the universe and the belief or approval of man. God is thus not to be viewed as an "it," but as a person.

God is the supreme Being who created the universe. He is not to be identified as any kind of impersonal force or energy. He has all the attributes of personality and thinks and feels and acts as a true person.

Monotheism says there is only one true God who is the Creator and Sustainer of the universe. The three great monotheistic faiths are Judaism, Christianity and Islam. Within these three religions and their respective bibles, man is called upon to worship the one true God who is a true person. God is not an impersonal force and man does not participate in God's essence or being and man never becomes a God himself.

Polytheism

The second kind of theism is traditionally called polytheism. This is the belief in many gods. Polytheism can be viewed in terms of a rather primitive animism in which the gods or spirits inhabit everything from tree stumps to animals. Polytheism is also the basis for the ancient Greco-Roman gods such as Zeus and Hercules who supposedly lived on Mount Olympus. It is also the basis for popular Hinduism which claims to worship over three billion gods. It is embraced by southern Buddhism which leads to the worship of many gods.

Many modern-day cults such as Mormonism and the Worldwide Church of God teach the doctrine of polytheism in that they believe that they can become gods and thus there is more than one god.

The Scriptures are clear in teaching that there is only true God by nature. There were no other gods before God. There are no other gods beside Him. And there will be no other gods after Him. He alone by nature is God. The following Scriptures clearly teach monotheism:

Isa. 43:10-13; 44:6-8; 45:5-5, 14, 21-22; 46:9; I Cor. 8:4-6; 10:19-20; Gal. 4:8-9; I Tim. 2:5; 6:15-16.

Polytheism cannot serve as a sufficient basis for truth, justice, morals or beauty because it cannot supply one single unifying principle for human society. The gods are immoral because they are involved in rape, murder, adultery, just as their human creators are involved in such things. There is constant conflict among the gods themselves. Some gods are good and some are evil. What is good for one god is evil to the next.

Polytheism has never produced a sufficient basis for an absolute standard in truth, justice or morals. It cannot work because we must appeal to a higher standard or higher being by which we are able to distinguish a good god from an evil god. It is to this higher being that the monotheists point as being the true and everlasting God.

Atheism is the denial of theism. There are two kinds of atheism: religious and secular.

Religious Atheism

In religious atheism we find such systems as pantheism, which is the belief that the universe and God are, for all practical purposes, identical. Pantheism thus denies that God has His own separate existence apart from the existence of the universe. For the pantheist, the world is God and God is the world. Or, as it is sometimes stated, all is God and God is all. Thus pantheism is a subtle form of atheism in that it denies the existence of a God who stands apart from and independent from the existence of the universe. Pantheists believe that what is, is God.

Pantheism serves as the philosophic base of classical Hinduism, northern Buddhism, Zen Buddhism, Christian Science, Unity, the "mind" cults and the New Age Movement. In its Eastern or Western forms, God is often reduced to an impersonal "it" which forms the basis of the universe. God is referred to as the "force" or "energy" which makes up the world.

Pantheism has always had a difficult time with the problem of evil. Since God is all and all is God and God is good and thus all is good, there is no room for the existence of evil! Pantheism in its Eastern or Western forms always ends up denying the existence of evil.

Because Pantheism denies the existence of evil, it cannot recognize the existence of human suffering. Regardless if one is dealing with a Hindu guru or a New Ager, they will both tell you that there is no such thing as evil, thus there is no such thing as pain or sickness. It is all in the mind. In order for there to be no such thing as pain, there is no such thing as a physical body. Thus they deny the existence of the material world in order to escape the problems of evil and human suffering. One such example would be "holistic medicine" in which the human mind is said to create sickness or health.

Secular Atheism

Secular atheism manifests itself in various philosophical and political systems based on the concept of materialism which is the belief that reality is limited to that which has a physical nature. If something cannot be weighed and measured, it is not capable of sensory knowledge and cannot really exist. Thus God, the soul or the mind do not exist because they are supposedly of an immaterial nature.

Pantheists and materialists represent two extremes. While pantheists deny the existence of matter and affirm the existence of the mind, materialists deny the existence of the mind and affirm the existence of matter! They reduce reality to either matter or mind.

Materialism cannot provide a sufficient basis for truth, justice, morals, meaning or beauty. It is thoroughly committed to an amoral universe in which there are no standards of righteousness, truth, or justice. Materialism always ends in relativism and skepticism.

It was in this sense that materialism functioned as the basis of Nazism and now functions as the basis of Marxism and Western secular humanism. Human beings are viewed only as a random collection of molecules and have no intrinsic worth, significance or meaning. We must remember that both the Third Reich and the USSR created a vast system of concentration camps where human life had no value.

One great example of materialism is B. F. Skinner's book

Beyond Freedom and Dignity. In this book, Skinner teaches that man should be viewed simply as an animal or a machine. Thus man does not have more dignity, worth or significance than a vacuum cleaner, a stone or a dog.

Materialism is philosophically absurd for it would have us believe that:

> "everything came from nothing, order came from chaos, harmony came from discord, life came from non-life, reason came from the non-rational, personality came from the non-personal, and morality came from the non-moral."

Materialism attempts to reduce all of life to the level of a stone or a tree stump. It cannot explain life as it is. It carries within itself the seeds of its own destruction when it says there is no such thing as an idea or a thought. If all "ideas" are simply chemical secretions of the brain, then materialism itself is only a secretion of the brain and is not to be viewed as being any more "true" than any other secretion of the brain. Any philosophic view, such as materialism, which refutes itself must be viewed with pity as well as disgust.

How to Talk With an Atheist

There are several different kinds of atheists. The kind of atheist which one traditionally runs into on a college or university campus is rather dogmatic and claims, "There is no God." This kind of atheist is emphatic in that he *knows* that God does not exist.

This atheist can be dealt with quickly. The only person who can say with confidence that there has never been and never will be a God of any shape or description in the universe is God Himself. In other words, the atheist would have to become God in order for him to say emphatically that there is no God!

To say that there is no God means that you must have been

everywhere at the same time throughout all of the past, present and future and can now state that you did not find any deity of any shape, size or description. In addition to being omnipresent, you would have to be omniscient or all-knowing. And, in order to be omniscient and omnipresent, you would have to be omnipotent. Thus the atheist in order to deny the existence of God would have to become God!

Another kind of atheist is what is traditionally called an "agnostic." There are two kinds of agnostics: ordinary and ornery.

An ordinary agnostic says, "I really don't know if God exists or not. If you can show me enough evidence of His existence I will accept the fact that He exists."

An ornery agnostic says, "I don't know if God exists. You don't know if God exists. Nobody can know if God exists."

When someone says, "God is unknowable" or "God cannot be known," they are giving a self-refuting statement. The only way that someone could say that God's existence is unknowable is that he knows everything about God. Thus the claim that God is unknowable is irrational.

It is also irrational when agnostics assume that if they do not know if God exists, then no one else can know. The attributes of a part cannot be attributed to the whole. Just because they are ignorant of God does not logically imply that everyone else is ignorant.

The typical logical fallacies used by atheists and agnostics are examined in Dr. Morey's book, *The New Atheism and the Erosion of Freedom* (Crowne Publications, Mass., Rep. 1989). Every student should have a copy of this book before heading off to college.

The ornery agnostic is actually a covert atheist who has been forced by smart theists to admit that traditional atheism is a philosophic absurdity. The attempt to prove a universal negative, namely that God does not exist, is a hopeless and fruitless task. This is why some atheists pretend to be agnostics.

It is interesting to note that the word "agnostic" comes from the Greek word which means ignorant or ignoramus.

Most ornery agnostics are quite dogmatic about what they know even though the term which they use to describe themselves — agnostic — means that they do not know anything at all! A true agnostic cannot decide ahead of time what is or is not knowable.

An agnostic is someone who claims that he is open to the existence of God if God's existence can be demonstrated to him in ways that he finds acceptable. The key to this kind of mentality is that all proofs must be "acceptable" to him. Thus whenever you give him a sound evidence for the existence of God based upon human reason or experience, he can get out of it by simply stating that it is not "acceptable" to him. This is why you can chase such agnostics from argument to argument never finding anything that stops them for one moment. They rationalize any evidence that is presented to them.

One example of this kind of procedure is the attempt to deny the historicity of Jesus of Nazareth. Some modern agnostics make the claim that there is no evidence whatsoever that Jesus ever existed.

When one examines their arguments against the traditional evidence for the existence of Christ, one is left with the impression that no historical person's existence would be acceptable if the same standards were applied to them as are applied to Jesus. In this sense, one would have to deny the existence of Caesar Augustus or Abraham Lincoln as well as Jesus of Nazareth.

What we discover is that there is a double standard in operation. Some agnostics apply to the theistic proofs or the existence of Jesus standards of rationality or historicity which they are not willing to apply to any other subject or individual. This at once reveals that most of the arguments given by agnostics, skeptics and free thinkers against the existence of God, inspiration of the Bible and the historicity of Christ are actually based upon logical fallacies such as "special pleading." When they have to justify their arguments against Christianity, agnostics reveal that they do not have any arguments at all.

Summary

Christianity begins with the assumption of the existence of a God who is the Creator and Sustainer of the universe. The infinite God of the Bible provides a sufficient basis for truth, justice, morals, meaning and beauty. Only by beginning with the God of the Bible can man have any dignity, worth and significance.

A wonderful window of opportunity has opened for Christian students on secular campuses because humanistic philosophers have finally concluded that there can be no absolutes of any kind. Without absolutes there can be no morality, meaning or purpose to life. Thus they have nothing to offer students but skepticism and relativism. On the other hand, the only ones on campus who have a message of hope are the Christians. They alone stand for absolutes in truth and morals. They alone have meaning, dignity, worth and significance. Now is the time for them to be bold with the Gospel.

Diagram #1

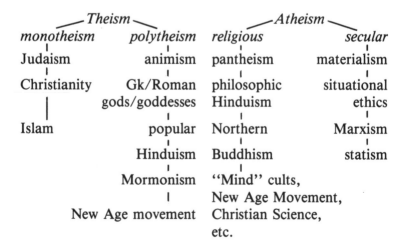

Questions for Discussion

1. Please explain the two basic kinds of theism.
2. In what way does monotheism provide an absolute standard for truth, morals, justice and beauty?
3. Can polytheism provide a sufficient base for truth, morals, justice or beauty?
4. What is animism?
5. How many gods are worshipped in India?
6. How is Mormonism related to Hinduism?
7. In what two forms does atheism manifest itself?
8. How is pantheism a subtle form of atheism?
9. How is Christian Science related to Hinduism?
10. Can you name any of the popular science of mind cults?
11. Can any religion based on pantheism cope with the twin problems of the existence of evil and human suffering?
12. Can the philosophy of materialism generate any truth or morals?
13. How would you answer someone who said, "I know that God does not exist"?
14. Why does materialism always lead to totalitarianism in forms of government?
15. If you begin with man instead of God, will you end in total despair and meaninglessness? Why is this?
16. If you begin with God, will you end with truth, morals, justice, beauty, significance and meaning? Why is this?

THREE

Know Thyself

What is your self-image? Do you view yourself as being limited or unlimited? Do you have an infinite potential to be whatever you want to be? Do you view yourself as being on the same level as a dog or a god?

The issue of a proper self-image is not only essential to an understanding of the nature of man in general but also essential to living a successful life. If you have a very poor self-image, this will cripple your attempt to be successful at anything you do. On the other hand, if you have an overrated self-image, this will produce frustration and perfectionism in that you will attempt to be and do things for which you are not equipped. This is why the apostle Paul urged us not to have too high or too low a view of ourselves (Rom. 12:3).

The Scriptures address the question "What is man?" in such places as Psalms 8:3-9.

> "When I consider your heavens, the work of your fingers, the moon and the stars, which you have set in place, what is man that you are mindful of him, the son of man that you care for him? You made him a little lower than the heavenly beings and crowned him with glory and honor. You made him ruler over the works of your hands; you put everything under his feet: all flocks and herds, and the beasts of the field, the birds of the air, and the fish of the sea, all that swim the paths of the seas. O Lord, our Lord, how majestic

is your name in all the earth!''

Throughout the history of philosophy, mankind has struggled with the issue of a proper self-image. Those who struggled with the issue without the aid of the Holy Scriptures invariably developed either too low or too high a view of man which always led to the loss of any dignity, worth, significance or meaning for human life.

Not only does our view of the nature of man affect our own self-image, but it also directly affects the way we look at economics, politics and society in general.

The Christian View of Reality
(God/Angels/Man/Animals/Things)

In the Christian world view, we begin with God for this is where the Bible begins (Gen. 1:1). God is placed first because He is the Creator and Sustainer of all of things.

The second category has to do with those beings which we generally call angels or spirits which God created to carry out His work. This class of beings encompasses all angels, good and bad.

The third category is that of man. Man is not God or even a part of God. Neither is man an angel. While the 19th Century romantic idea that people become angels when they die is the foundation of the *Book of Mormon*, the Bible knows nothing of such a concept.

Just as man is not to be confused with God or angels, neither is man to be viewed as an animal or a thing. While animals are creatures of God, they do not have an immortal soul. They were not made in the image of God like man.

The Christian world view also makes a distinction between animals and things. We must not treat animals as if they were only rocks or machines. This is why in such places as Pro. 12:10, we are told,

''A righteous man cares for the needs of his animal,

but the kindest acts of the wicked are cruel."

In the Christian system, man is placed above animals and things because as God's image bearer he was made the prophet, priest and king over all the earth. This is why he is called to take dominion over it.

> "Then God said, 'Let us make man in our image, in our likeness, and let them rule over the fish of the sea and the birds of the air, over the livestock, over all the earth, and over all the creatures that move along the ground.' "
>
> (Gen. 1:26)

In the Biblical view, mankind stands uniquely outside of nature. Man is not just one cog among many in the cosmic machine. He was given stewardship over the world. He has the unique responsibility of developing the world around him to its fullest potential to the glory of the God who made him.

The Humanistic View of Reality

In the non-Christian world view, we find a downward process that ultimately reduces everything to the category of "things." Once you deny the existence of the God revealed in Scriptures, there is no rational basis to believe in the existence of angels. Once you have done away with angelic beings, there is no reason to speak of "man" as if he were unique.

Since it is man's relationship to God as His image bearer that gives man dignity and meaning, once God is gone, man is reduced to being an animal. There is nothing to separate man from animal. Human beings can be viewed as cattle which can be bred, slaughtered and processed at will.

Lest someone think that this is not possible, let us remember that it has already been done. The Nazis' concentration camps used human hair to make cloth; human flesh to make soap; human skin to make pocketbooks, lamp shades, belts and wallets; and human bones to make fertilizer.

The Communists in Russia, China, Vietnam, Cambodia, Cuba, etc., do the same things in principle with their slave labor camps. They have already slaughtered over 150 million people in the 20th Century. Human life is always cheap in non-Christian cultures.

But once you have reduced everything to animal life there is no reason to make a distinction between animals and objects such as rocks. Thus man can be treated as if he had no more significance than a tree stump!

This is the exact position of such totalitarian views as Marxism. Man is viewed as a commodity which either benefits or detracts from the state. People may be murdered at will because they have no more significance than dogs or cats. This is why the Russians starved to death over 5 million Ukrainians, the Cambodian Communists murdered over one half of the population of their country, and the Ethiopian Communists starved to death over half of their people.

The Marxists have murdered millions of people without any sense of guilt because to them people are only *things* and thus they do not have any intrinsic worth, significance, meaning, dignity or freedom.

If you view yourself as being only an animal, you will live and die as an animal. If you view yourself as only a machine, you will live and die as a machine. But if you view yourself as uniquely created to bear God's image and as being called upon to take dominion of this world for the glory of God, then you will live life to its fullest because you will have dignity, worth, significance, meaning and freedom.

Let us examine some of the false views of man that have generated defective self-images which cripple people and limit them from reaching the potential that God planned.

Too Low a View of Man

In those views which have too low a view of man, man is reduced to the level of an animal, a machine or a thing. This has great significance for such things as human rights and civil rights.

At one time, humanistic thought decreed that black people were animals and should not be viewed or treated as human beings with dignity, worth or freedom. The Supreme Court at that time in a famous case backed up these humanists by ruling that the Negro was only an animal and hence a "thing" which can be purchased, sold or bartered at will.

What modern humanists failed to mention to their students is that they now believe that all people regardless of race are only animals and no one has an immortal soul. Thus totalitarian forms of government arise in which people are viewed as "slaves of the state." There are no intrinsic, civil or human rights because man is only an animal. Man as *man* doesn't have any more "rights" than a groundhog.

In some cases, certain animals have more "rights" than man! We are living in a time when it is a crime to destroy the egg of an eagle or to kill a baby seal but unborn human children can be slaughtered at will! While animal rights activists protest against the use of animals in medical experiments, they suggest using human beings instead! Man is now lower than the animals!

The only basis for human rights or civil rights as expressed in the American founding articles is that there is a supreme Creator who endowed man with certain inalienable rights. These rights are given to man from his Creator and not from the state. The state cannot take away what God has given. Thus man is viewed as having dignity, worth, significance, freedom and meaning because of the existence of the God who made him.

Not only is the dignity of man dependent upon the Judeo-Christian concept of a Creator who invests man with certain inalienable rights, but also the unity of mankind itself is based upon the Biblical model of Adam and Eve being the original parents of the entire human race.

While evolutionists teach that the different races developed from different primate ancestries and hence are not developed from a single pair, Christians believe that all of mankind ultimately came from Adam and Eve. The unity of mankind depends on racial solidarity and a common ancestry. Once you reject the Adam and Eve model of the book of Genesis, you have opened the door for racism.

One such example of racism was the Nazis' glorification of the Aryan race. They believed that the Aryan race was the superior race which would ultimately produce the "super man." In the light of this commitment to racism, the Germans sought to purify the genetic basis of the Aryan stock by murdering countless millions of Jews, gypsies and other minority racial groups.

It is no surprise to find leaders connected with planned parenthood and professors in leading Ivy League colleges and universities who openly teach racism. They have gone on record as teaching that certain racial groups such as blacks be sterilized to prevent them from genetically reproducing their own kind. It is argued that if man is only an animal, then the state should have the right to weed out inferior individuals and entire races.

Another subtle form of racism which has been produced by the idea that man is only an animal, is that childbearing should be controlled by the state and the state should limit reproduction to those who meet various IQ tests or other qualifications.

Man is viewed as an animal which needs to be controlled in order to breed out undesirable qualities. This is the hidden agenda of such books as Skinner's *Beyond Freedom and Dignity,* or Orwell's *1984.*

Once you come to the position that man is only an animal kicked up by a meaningless chance-controlled evolutionary process which is not going anywhere for there is no predetermined plan or goal, you can accept such things as:

> abortion: the murder of unborn children for the sake of convenience or pleasure.
> infanticide: the murder of small children who are in the way of one's pursuit of personal pleasure.

mercy killing: the murder of handicapped or terminally ill patients for economic reasons
euthanasia: the murder of the elderly in order to
seize their properties and possessions.

The view that man is only an animal means the loss of dignity, worth, significance, meaning and freedom for humanity. Once you come to the conclusion that God is dead, you are driven to the conclusion that man is dead as well.

Too High a View of Man

In opposition to the low view of man which is taught by secular humanists, there are those who are involved in religious forms of humanism which teach a view of man that is too high.

Instead of man being reduced to the level of a dog, they elevate man to the level of a god. They have eaten the forbidden fruit of Genesis 3, which is the great lie that man can become a god.

Man is elevated to godhood by investing him with the attributes and powers that belong only to the Creator of the universe. Just as God created the universe by speaking it into being, man is said to be able to speak his own world into being as well.

Man's potential and power are said to be infinite. He is said to participate in the being and essence of God or to have flowed out of God and is in the process of flowing back into God. It is claimed that man's powers are infinite and absolute. Man can be and do whatever he wants to be or do.

This absurd view of man was taught by the Hinduism for thousands of years. It was introduced into the West during the later part of the 19th Century and has been popularized by all the Hindu gurus that have come to the West seeking their fortunes. One look at the filth, poverty and ignorance of Eastern countries reveals what such a false view of man produces in the lives of those who believe it.

The idea that man is a god is also taught by those involved in the New Age movement. One actress went so far as to claim to be God on national TV! Others speak of the "infinite" potential of every human being. They would have us believe that we are sick only because we think we are sick. We can be healthy, wealthy or wise if we only will it or wish it into being.

This is also the basis of the present fad of parapsychology and ESP experimentation. It is believed that man has "hidden" powers and that he can develop them through ESP. It is hoped that through parapsychology people will be able to develop their infinite potential as little gods to create and control the world around them.

One form of this new godism is what is popularly called "positive thinking." Norman Vincent Peale, the father of positive thinking, has revealed in his autobiography that he derived some of his concepts from such "mind" cults as Unity, Theosophy, Science of the mind, Christian Science, etc.

In each of these cults, man is viewed as being the creator of his own world. In other words, man is his own god and is not in need of God's grace or revelation. Man is self-sufficient and can create his own world through his own inherent powers.

Even some Christian groups have fallen into this form of godism. They would have us believe that we can be whatever we want to be and do whatever we want to do if we simply claim it, name it, pray it, or speak it into being. Instead of attributing Creation to the power of God, they claim that God had to tap into the power of "faith" to do it. In other words, God didn't create anything at all. It was the power of "faith" that created the world. Faith is viewed as the omnipotent power which all of us can utilize to create our own worlds. Thus God is pushed out of the universe and is no longer needed for "by faith" we can get whatever we want without Him.

The Christian View of Man

The Biblical world view interprets all of life in terms of three basic ideas:

1. The Creation of the universe out of nothing.
2. The Fall of man into sin and judgment.
3. The Redemption accomplished by Christ.

In Christian philosophy, we refer to these three principles as Creation, Fall and Redemption. They are the basis of all Christian thinking. This is why they are introduced at the very beginning of the Bible in Genesis 1-3. The rest of Scripture is a development and application of these three concepts to all of life. Just like a three legged stool, remove one of these principles and Christianity falls.

A Scriptural self-image begins with an application of Creation, Fall and Redemption to the nature of man.

Creation

First, in terms of Creation, man is not to be viewed as an animal or machine but as a unique creature created in the image of God. As such man is to be viewed as something wonderful and not as junk.

Man has been invested by his Creator with certain inalienable rights which no one, not even the state, should violate. Man is a free moral agent who has not been programmed deterministically by anything in the world around him. This means that man is responsible for his actions and will be held accountable on the Day of Judgment for how he lived his life.

When you look in a mirror you can say to yourself,

"I have been created in the image of God and I have worth, significance, meaning and dignity. I have freedom to develop my potential according to the glory of God and to take dominion of the world around me."

Fall

In terms of the Fall, when we look in the mirror we see ourselves as sinners who have rebelled against the God who made us.

Man was given the choice of either obeying or rebelling against God. In Genesis 3, man followed the advice of Satan and rebelled against God and plunged the entire human race into guilt and depravity. This means that we are sinners by nature and sin comes quite naturally to us (Rom. 5:12-19).

The radical nature of the Fall explains the darker side of man's nature. How can such wonderful creatures, beautifully constructed by God with such great potential, do such horrible things? Where does human evil come from? Why do men do the evil they do?

When you look at a mirror you can say to yourself,

"I am a sinner in need of God's grace and forgiveness. I have broken God's laws and deliberately transgressed His commandments. I will one day stand before God on the Judgment Day to give an account of every thought, word and deed."

Redemption

The third concept by which the Scriptures interpret all of life is the concept of Redemption. As we have demonstrated in *The Saving Work of Christ,* God did not leave man in the state of sin, guilt, misery and condemnation. Instead, He sent His Son to do a work of redemption by which not only man but also the world will be redeemed from the evil consequences of the Fall (John 3:16; Rom. 8:19-22).

Salvation or redemption is not to be viewed in terms of absorption or annihilation. When God saves an individual, that person will not be absorbed into God's essence or being. As redeemed individuals we will exist for all eternity.

The atonement is the payment of the price demanded by Justice in order to set us free from the just condemnation of our sins. Christ Jesus has done all that is necessary for our salvation. Our responsibility is simply to receive His wonderful work of salvation (John 1:12). Thus salvation is by the grace of God and it is not based on human merit, performance or work (Eph. 2:8, 9).

Not only is the soul of man redeemed so that after death he can live in the presence of God in heaven, but his body will be redeemed at the Resurrection (I Thess. 5:23). Thus man and his world are to be redeemed and purified by the Creator through the saving work of Jesus Christ.

God's plan of salvation gives us the solution to the problem of evil. Evil is going to be assessed and brought to judgment one day and then quarantined in a place called hell where it can never again affect the rest of the universe. All of the evil consequences of sin will be eradicated by God's work of redemption. Mankind and his world will be purified from all the effects of Adam's fall into sin.

The work of Christ is thus the final answer to the problem of evil. Evil will be dealt with either by redemption or judgment. Christ has triumphed over sin and will one day bring the universe back into its original harmony and beauty (Col. 1:18-20).

If you are a Christian, when you look in the mirror, you can say to yourself,

> "I am a child of God through faith in the atoning work of Jesus Christ. I have been saved by grace alone, through faith alone, through Christ alone. He is my Savior and my God. I now trust in Him for all things and live only to please Him."

The Christian position on the nature of man involves three foundational concepts: We are wonderfully created in the image of God, terribly marred and twisted by the fall and marvelously redeemed by the atonement of Christ. Any anthropology which does not take into account the threefold state of man in terms of Creation, Fall and Redemption is not a Christian or biblical perspective.

The threefold biblical view of man's nature in which he is viewed as an image bearer, a sinner and a saint provides us with a sufficient basis not only to develop a proper self-image but also to develop a free society.

The authors of the American Constitution believed that man was a sinner by nature and thus he needed a system of checks and balances for government to work. They believed that power corrupts and that absolute power corrupts absolutely. Therefore no branch of the government is to gain the supremacy over the other branches of the government. By its system of checks and balances, totalitarianism and tyranny can be prevented in this great land.

Capitalism and the free market system developed out of the Christian view of man. A planned economy has always led to utter disaster. Countries which have gone into Marxism cannot even feed themselves. Without the free economies of the West, these countries would have gone down in ruin years ago.

The only hope of humanity is to return to the Christian view of man and to the principles of form and freedom, dignity and worth that have been generated by the Christian system. The only alternative is totalitarianism which treats man only as a thing.

Diagram #2

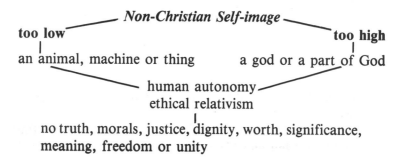

abortion, infanticide, mercy killing, suicide, euthanasia, racism, genetic engineering

statism, socialism, Marxism, Fascism, totalitarianism

death of a culture

Diagram #3

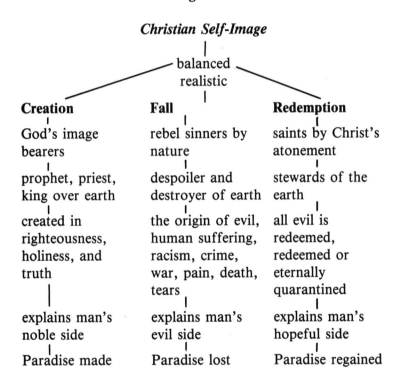

Christian Self-Image

balanced
realistic

Creation	**Fall**	**Redemption**
God's image bearers	rebel sinners by nature	saints by Christ's atonement
prophet, priest, king over earth	despoiler and destroyer of earth	stewards of the earth
created in righteousness, holiness, and truth	the origin of evil, human suffering, racism, crime, war, pain, death, tears	all evil is redeemed, redeemed or eternally quarantined
explains man's noble side	explains man's evil side	explains man's hopeful side
Paradise made	Paradise lost	Paradise regained

Summary

The healthiest self-image is the one derived from Scripture because it describes man as he really is. Thus there is no contradiction between what we experience in life and what we find in the Bible. Man and his world are understandable only if we look at them from the perspective of Creation, Fall and Redemption. Any other world view is doomed to fail.

Questions for Discussion

1. Is it possible to have too low or too high a view of man?
2. How will a wrong view of man affect your self-image?
3. Does a proper self-image have anything to do with success in life?
4. As a Christian, where should you obtain your self-image?
5. If you view man as being only an animal, what consequences will result in society?
6. On what concept is abortion, infanticide, mercy killing and euthanasia based?
7. How would you answer someone who said that abortion, infanticide, mercy killing, euthanasia, genetic engineering and racism were perfectly proper because man was only an animal?
8. Have you encountered individuals who believed that man is a god or can become a god or is a part of god? What would you say to them?
9. The idea of human autonomy is that man is self-sufficient and is not in need of God's grace or revelation. Thus man can discover truth, morals, justice and beauty without God's word. Is this really possible?
10. Ethical relativism is the idea that there are no absolute standards for truth, justice, morals or beauty but each person is to develop his own standards. Can such a view lead to a just and orderly society or will it result in anarchy?
11. What are the implications of man being created in the image of God?
12. From whom do our "inalienable rights" come? Is it correct to say that the Constitution gives us rights or that it only recognizes those rights we already have from the Creator?

13. What significance does the radical fall into sin have for mankind in general and man's political structure for government in particular?
14. Is God interested only in the saving of the soul or does salvation include the body and the world?
15. How will Jesus Christ solve the problem of evil?

FOUR

Getting the Essentials Down

Going to college for many young people means that for the first time in their life they must deal with a world which is quite hostile to Christianity without the support of their family, friends, or church. They enter a time of testing in which it will be revealed if they are really saved.

One of the most important aspects of spiritual survival on a college campus is to keep in mind the essentials of the Christian life. The first signs of apostasy or falling away from the Lord are always found in the abandonment of the essentials of the Christian life.

We have seen it far too often. Within a semester or two, many professing Christian students stop reading the Bible, praying, going to church, attending Christian campus groups or witnessing. By their senior year they either openly deny the Gospel or try to deceive their parents by attending church when they are home on the holidays. How can they walk away from the claims of the Gospel?

The key is to realize that their religion was something *external* to them.

Their profession of salvation was the result of the external influences of a Christian home and church. Because there was no true Christianity in their hearts, once the external pressures of home and church were removed, they reverted to their natural pagan state. As soon as they were in a situation where they did not *have* to go to church, they stopped going.

But what if we go to a Christian college? Will this solve the problem? What often surprises students is that they can lose their faith at a Christian college as quickly as they can lose their faith at a state university or college. Why is this true?

Campus life gives students the opportunity to reveal what is really in their heart of hearts. If they love the things of the world and they view college time as "party time," they will party regardless if they are at a Christian or secular college. They will be involved in immorality and drugs regardless if they are attending an evangelical or state school. What is in their hearts will ultimately come out (Mark 7:21-23).

Going to a Christian college does not guarantee that you will keep the faith because the temptations to sin will be there. While the Christian atmosphere will put a damper on open wickedness, you can still find it if you look hard enough. You must not make the mistake of thinking that the external environment of a Christian college will automatically keep you from apostasy.

As a professing Christian, you should desire to retain your faith during your college years. Your parents and your pastor are also concerned that you survive all the spiritual tests, trials and temptations that one faces on a college campus. Only a fool would not seriously consider the possibility of apostasy. Surveys have clearly demonstrated that almost 75% of freshmen who profess to be Christians abandon Christianity by their senior year. Make sure that your faith is a true saving faith. You need to *possess* salvation as well as profess it. If you are truly converted you will endure unto the end (Matt. 24:13).

The warnings of the New Testament concerning the possibility of apostasy should be taken at face value. Apostasy concerns the falling away of *professing* Christians from their belief and obedience to the Scriptures. All theological systems recognize that *professing* Christians can fall away. This happens far too often during their college years.

We can claim to be saved only as long as we are living and believing according to Scripture. If we deny the doctrines of the Gospel or disobey God's law, we do not have the right to call ourselves "Christians."

> "By this gospel you are saved, *if* you hold firmly to the word I preached to you. Otherwise, you have believed in vain."
>
> (I Cor. 15:2)

> "But now he has reconciled you by Christ's physical body through death, *if* you continue in your faith, established and firm, not moved from the hope held out in the gospel."
>
> (Col. 1:22-23)

> "But Christ is faithful as a son over God's house. And we are his house, *if* we hold on to our courage and the hope of which we boast."
>
> (Heb. 3:6)

> "See to it, brothers, that none of you has a sinful, unbelieving heart that turns away from the living God. . . . We have come to share in Christ *if* we hold firmly till the end the confidence we had at first."
>
> (Heb. 3:12, 14)

> "The one who says, 'I have come to know Him,' and does not keep His commandments, is a *liar,* and the truth is not in him."
>
> (I John 2:4)

All professing Christians must take care that they do not "fall from grace" (Gal. 5:4). There were people in Christ's own day who claimed to be His disciples and yet they turned away from Him (John 6:66). Did not Jesus reveal that some of His disciples were not really saved but were in reality the "children of the devil" (John 8:31-47)? There were many people who at one point had made a profession of faith and then they departed from the Church never to return (I John 2:19).

We should all be concerned about our salvation. Is it real or a sham? How can you survive college with your Christianity intact? This is a very reasonable and rational question. These are the kinds of questions which you must ask yourself in order to prepare yourself for all the trials and temptations you will face in life.

What is the most important thing you can do to survive the spiritual temptations and trials of college life? You must persevere in the private and public means of grace.

What do we mean when we speak of the "means of grace"? The "means of grace" simply refer to those activities which help us to grow in the Christian life. Such things as daily Bible reading, praying, church attendance and Christian fellowship have always been the mainstays of the Christian life.

If we abandon the private and public means of grace, we no longer have any Biblical warrant to claim that we are Christians. It is thus absolutely essential that we continue to do those things which build up our faith and strengthen our submission to the Lordship of Christ (Col. 2:6-8).

1. Daily Bible Reading

The reading of the Bible is essential for the Christian life. In Acts 20:32, we are told that the Word of God is the "word of grace" which will enable us to grow.

We will never be able to develop Christian character if we are not reading about Christ in the Scriptures. This is why in such passages as Psalm 1 or Psalm 119, the reading of Scripture is seen as the primary influence on developing godliness in the life. It is the reading and meditation on Scripture that brings success and prosperity in the Christian life (Josh. 1:8).

The reading of the Bible is essential for the "renewing of the mind" (Rom. 12:2). We need to understand God, the world, ourselves and the issues of life. This is why the apostle Paul stated that the purpose of Scripture is to equip the child of God so that he is ready to handle anything that comes his way (II Tim. 3:16-17).

One of the most important aspects of the reading of Scripture is that it must be done *daily*. This can be most effectively done by assigning yourself a chapter in the book of Proverbs which corresponds to the day of the month. For example, on the 5th day of the month, read the 5th chapter of Proverbs. This means that you will be reading through the book of Proverbs every month.

We emphasize the reading of Proverbs because it was specifically written for young people to teach them wisdom and understanding. Wisdom is the ability to look at issues from God's perspective as given in Scripture. Understanding is the application of God's wisdom to a specific problem.

Proverbs helps you to identify certain kinds of people that you should avoid at all costs: fools, sluggards, scoffers, scoundrels, skeptics, con-men, and immoral people. Proverbs equips young people to escape temptation and sin by utilizing the principles of successful living found in God's Word. Everyone should read and apply Proverbs to life every day.

In addition to reading a chapter of Proverbs every day, it would be helpful to read one other chapter of Scripture. It is important to alternate between reading a chapter from the New Testament and a chapter from the Old Testament. In this way you balance the Law and Gospel, the old covenant and the new covenant.

In addition to a daily reading of Scripture, you should be doing detailed studies in the Scriptures. It can be a doctrine or a principle of the Christian life. You can do this in a Bible study group or you can do this by yourself. But the important thing is that you are meditating on Biblical truth.

Although college life can be very exciting and full of activities, it is important that you retain a portion of time for yourself. This is the time that you set aside for the development of your own spiritual and intellectual life. Take dominion of your life and set apart a specific time in which you will devote yourself to the reading of Scripture. Make notes as you read. Write papers on various subjects. In other words, use the mind that God gave you to search the Scriptures daily (Acts 17:11).

2. Prayer

As you read the Scriptures, you find an emphasis on prayer. We are given such examples as Enoch who "walked with God" (Gen. 5:22). What does it mean to "walk with God"?

Walking with God means that you are living a life in which whenever your mind is free from its responsibilities, it naturally and immediately flies to the presence of God like a homing pigeon. It means that whenever you are faced with a trial or temptation you immediately go to prayer and ask God for wisdom and grace. In this way, you fulfill the Biblical command that we "should always pray and not give up" (Lk. 18:1). Your goal as a Christian is to walk with God every day.

In addition to developing a prayerful attitude, you need to set apart specific times in which you will devote yourself to prayer. You need to pray for the family that you have left behind and for your home church. You need to pray about your friends. You need to pray about class assignments, upcoming tests, opportunities of ministry and opportunities of witnessing to the faculty and fellow students.

A true Christian always complains that he does not have enough time to pray and that there are too many things to pray about. A "Christian" student who does not pray because he cannot think of anything to pray about is probably not saved. A prayerless person is a Christless person.

Once God has given someone a new heart, he will instinctively pray to the God who saved him. This is how Ananias was assured that Saul of Tarsus was truly converted. God told Ananias, "Behold, he prayeth!" (Acts 9:11).

3. Christian Books

In addition to reading your Bible and to praying, your years at college provide you with the opportunity to develop a solid Christian perspective on all the academic subjects you are studying. Regardless if you are at a state university or a Christian college, you have a God-given responsibility to discover what the Bible says about history, psychology, physics, science, economics, political science, math, comparative religion, etc.

For the most part, you will never be assigned books which will give you the Christian position. Even on Christian campuses you will usually be given the same secular textbooks used in state universities. This is regrettable but true because most Christian colleges have never developed a distinctively Christian perspective on the subjects they teach. It is assumed that it is "Christian" education because the teacher utters a prayer before he teaches. A Christian college should teach every subject from a biblical perspective. This is rarely the case.

Even though this means that you will have to read more books than are assigned to you by your professor, it will pay off in the long run. Instead of filling your mind with false ideas and concepts which you must shed as fast as you can in order to retain your faith, your years at college will provide you with the opportunity of developing a Christian perspective on all of life. A special bibliography is given at the end of this book which will provide you with some solid Christian books to read.

In addition to reading Christian perspective books such as written by Francis Schaeffer, it would be good if you read Christian books that deal with growth in the Christian life, evangelism, biblical studies, theology and philosophy. You should also read good biographies which set before you examples of godly men and women who affected their generation in a real way.

In short, you need to read, read and read. Then you must think, think and think again if you are going to succeed and excel to greatness. You must understand what Christianity is all about and how it applies to all of life. Since non-Christian professors will not give you this understanding, you will have to get it yourself.

4. Church Attendance

In terms of the public means of grace, the first sign of apostasy is when a professing Christian stops attending church while at college. All kinds of rationalizations are given. But a rationalization is only a lie stuffed into the skin of an excuse and served up as the truth.

Some students claim that they stopped going to church because they need their sleep Sunday morning. Other students point to exams or papers that are due on Monday and argue that Sunday must be a day of study and preparation. Some students do not attend church because there is not a church "good" enough for them. Whatever the rationalization, these students gradually come to the habit of never attending church while they are away at college. They have fallen away from the Faith.

In the New Testament we are taught that church attendance is not optional for Christians.

> "Let us not give up meeting together, as some are in the habit of doing, but let us encourage one another — and all the more as you see the Day approaching."
>
> (Heb. 10:25)

The Scriptures view those who stop attending church as being apostates, i.e., no longer Christians (I John 2:19). A true child of God will seek out the fellowship of the saints (Mal. 3:16-18). The New Testament knows nothing of a churchless Christian any more than it knows of a prayerless Christian.

How does one go about choosing a church to attend? If you are away from your home church, the first step is to ask your pastor if he knows of a church he can recommend to you. Perhaps your parents have a friend in the area who attends a good church. If you have to find a church on your own, there are several things which you should be looking for in the churches you try. Any church which fails the following tests should be avoided.

1. Is there a commitment to the supremacy of Scripture? Is the full inspiration and inerrancy of Scripture clearly taught by this church? Does the pastor believe that the Scriptures alone are to decide all issues of doctrine and life?

2. Does this church clearly teach that salvation is based

solely on the unmerited grace of God? Is salvation by grace alone, through faith alone, in Christ alone? Any church which does not openly teach that the grace of God is the sole foundation of salvation is not a true Christian church.

3. Does this church discipline its membership? If a member of the congregation falls into sin, is this person dealt with lovingly but firmly according to the biblical principles?

4. Does this church have a proper view of baptism and the Lord's supper? Do they view these things as means by which we can be saved or as magical ceremonies? Any church which views baptism or the Lord's supper in a superstitious way or as being a magical ceremony which saves or sanctifies is not a true Christian church.

5. Does this church practice the biblical principle of "Body Life"? Body Life means that the church is committed to the priesthood of every believer. This means that the church is not a one man show staged by a super pastor. Do the members of this congregation seek to minister to each other according to the gifts that God has given to them? Is there an emphasis upon the ministry that God has given to all the members of the church?

6. Is this church involved in dynamic and biblical worship? Are its services God-centered or man-centered? Do people attend church to be entertained or to worship God? Is there the awareness of the presence of God that draws you to His throne?

7. Are the members of this church actively involved in personal evangelism? Is the church as a whole interested in missions? Is there an emphasis upon winning people to Christ?

8. Does this church have a social conscience? Is the Lordship of Christ applied to all of life? Is this church involved in applying the Bible to such subjects as politics, war, economics, abortion, mercy killing or euthanasia? Is this church opposed to secular humanism? Are they ministering to the poor and needy?

While these eight signs will not be found in perfection in any church, any sound gospel church will manifest these things to some degree. Such a church will deepen your faith in the

Lord Jesus Christ, strengthen your love toward the brethren and encourage your hope in the Scriptures as God's absolute and final authority.

5. Christian Activities on Campus

God never intended for you to go it alone on the college campus. You will need the fellowship of other Christians on campus. If there isn't a Christian group already in existence, then you should start one. Begin a Bible study in your dorm.

There are many excellent campus ministries such as Inter-Varsity or Campus Crusade for Christ. Perhaps one of these groups has already formed a group on your campus. If not, contact them about setting something up. It is essential that you do not attempt to go it alone.

One of the benefits of being involved with Christian groups on campus is that they can watch over your soul. If you begin to slip in your Christian life, they will exhort you and lead you back to repentance.

It is also helpful to know other Christians majoring in the same subjects that you are studying. Some of them may have already done research on a Christian perspective on your major and will be happy to share with you the principles of God's Word concerning that academic subject. There is no reason for you to "reinvent the wheel." Older and more experienced Christians will be able to refer you to books which give the Christian perspective on important topics.

6. Campus Activities

One of the mistakes that many students make is to be defensive when they go to college. They feel threatened and attacked on all sides and therefore withdraw into a shell. This defeatist attitude is in violation of God's call to take dominion and rule over all of life (Gen. 1:28).

Instead of being on the defensive, Christian students should be on the offensive. Since they have everything going for them, they should not be burdened with an inferiority complex. They have a God who is greater than the gods of the heathen and who provides truth, meaning, justice, morals, worth, dignity and beauty.

In contrast, the humanists are utterly bankrupt when it comes to any subject requiring truth, justice or morals. They are the ones who should be put to shame today as they admit that they have nothing to offer mankind.

Christians have the high ground in life. Thus they should take dominion over all campus activities that are available to them. They should not sit on the sidelines of life under the mistaken notion that doing nothing is true spirituality. They must be involved in those activities which can form a base to mold the thinking of the student body such as campus newspapers, clubs, sports, theatre, etc.

This means that Christian students must view themselves as radical rebels for Christ. Instead of rebelling against Christianity as the humanists do, Christian students should be rebelling against humanism. It does not matter if the humanism that they rebel against is found in a Christian college or a state university. Humanism is humanism regardless if it is taught by a professing Christian or by someone who is openly anti-Christian.

One caution must be given. Being a rebel for Christ does not mean that we should be obnoxious, arrogant or disrespectful to those over us. We are referring to an intellectual rebellion in which you refuse to accept humanistic teaching. You can be respectful and disagree with your professors at the same time.

Taking dominion means that you will attempt insofar as your abilities allow to take over those aspects of campus life that can influence your school for Christ. For example, Christians should be actively involved in all the media expressions of their school. They should get on the school newspaper or work their way into the university television or radio station. Once they have worked their way into the structure then they can begin to give a distinctively Christian perspective on relevant issues such as drugs, AIDS, sex, abortion, etc.

What if the humanists say that Christians should not be allowed to speak out? Point out that the Constitution gives you the freedom of speech and the freedom of the press just like anyone else. Threaten to take them to court if they violate the Civil Rights Amendment by discrimination against you on the basis of creed. Do not take it lying down.

Those with artistic abilities should take dominion of the cultural activities on campus. If you are an artist, seek to dominate art shows, art committees or art clubs. If you have musical ability, get involved in musicals or the campus orchestra. If you have a dramatic flair, be involved in plays or the production of campus skits.

One way to influence students is to write a play which ridicules humanism and its policy of death, such as abortion or euthanasia. Do what you can to take dominion of the entertainment to be produced and staged at the university.

One great way to influence your college or university is to arrange for a showing of Francis Schaeffer's film series such as *How Then Shall We Live?* Arrange for the entire student body to see it. Have your philosophy or ethics class view it.

Be involved in political action and get on the student government. Win the highest office you can. Don't be intimidated or afraid but aggressively seek to take dominion of the student government. In one college, a dedicated group of Christian students took over the student organization and then were able to influence the entire student body.

Join those campus clubs related to your major or to some hobby that you have. Or start your own club. Regardless of what the club is, be it a French or philosophy club, not only attend but seek to take dominion over it for Christ.

Why do so many students think that the "Christian" thing to do is to do nothing? Why do they let the humanists bully them? Why are they so passive? Why don't they demand their civil rights to speak out on issues? Why do they allow the humanists to ridicule God and the Bible openly in class? They are paralyzed by the false idea that they are not to be involved in the "world." They are so afraid of the world that they never try to clean it up!

We have a responsibility according to Scripture to apply the Lordship of Christ to all of life (II Cor. 10:5). Therefore Christian students must be at the forefront of all fights for truth, justice, morals and beauty.

For example, Christian students should be involved in actively supporting the human rights of the unborn, the sick and the elderly. These human rights are inalienable because they have been given by the Creator. Christian students should be involved in pro-life demonstrations and activities. They should actively support the showing of such films as *Silent Scream* or Francis Schaeffer's *Whatever Happened to the Human Race?*

Christians should be the most dedicated activists on earth. This is the Biblical ideal for every Christian. The Apostles won the reputation that they "were the men who turned the world upside down" (Acts 17:6). Indeed, wherever the early Christians went, riots and demonstrations were soon to follow. The greatest enemies to Christianity are those who preach, "Peace at any price," "Don't make any waves" and "Go with the flow."

Some Christian students are afraid that if they stand up for Christ, they will not be "popular." If they apply the Lordship of Christ to all of life and openly fight for Christianity, their professors and fellow students may not "like" them.

What these popularity seekers do not understand is that Jesus placed a curse on any one who lives for popularity. In Lk. 6:26, Jesus said,

> "Woe to you when all men speak well of you, for that
> is how their fathers treated the false prophets."

If you are ashamed of Jesus Christ and will not acknowledge His Lordship in the presence of men, then neither will He acknowledge you on the Day of Judgement (Matt. 10:32, 33).

Christians have received their marching orders from Jesus Christ (Matt. 28:18-20). They are under authority to aggressively go into the world and take dominion (Lk. 14:23).

Does this mean that every Christian student is also a missionary? Of course it does! You are either a missionary or a mission field. You are either a rebel for Christ or a rebel against Christ. You are either gathering with Christ or you are scattering against Christ. You cannot be neutral. If you are not actively for Christ, then you are against Him.

There is no neutrality with Jesus. Either you are for Him all the way, or not at all. He is either Lord of all or not Lord at all.

> "He who is not with me is against me, and he who does not gather with me scatters."
>
> (Matt. 12:30)

All of these things may seem to be very radical to some students because they have a soft Christianity. But now is the time to develop a tough Christianity that takes God and His Word seriously. Only a tough Christianity can survive and triumph in the secular world.

Even though you may have never seriously considered the biblical truth that we are to be "overcomers" (I John 5:4, 5), it is nevertheless true that God has called us to take dominion over this world (Gen. 1:26-28).

If the Christians of the last two generations had fought to win their world for Christ, we would not be in the terrible fix we find ourselves in today. We must not allow evil to overcome good but use the good to overcome evil (Rom. 12:21).

Summary

Will you commit yourself to be a rebel for Christ? Will you take that step of faith and determine within yourself that you are going to apply the Lordship of Christ to all of life? Are you prepared to pay any price for your allegiance to Jesus Christ? Are you going to obey God's command to take dominion? Perhaps the following prayer will help to seal your dedication to become an overcomer.

> "Lord Jesus, I acknowledge your Lordship over all of life. I ask that you will give me the wisdom and the humility to apply Your Lordship to every issue. Give me zeal and boldness to proclaim your Word. Give me the grace I need to be an overcomer."

Questions for Discussion

1. What are the essentials of the Christian life?
2. How important is prayer and Bible reading to a Christian? Is it possible to be a "prayerless" Christian?
3. Is church attendance optional or necessary for a valid profession of faith? Can someone be a "churchless" Christian?
4. How important is it to find good Christian books on the subjects you are studying?
5. Should you get involved with Christian groups on campus? Is someone really a Christian if he avoids any contact with Christians?
6. Should you seek to take dominion of the school where you are studying? Should you be defensive or offensive?
7. Should you be involved in cultural or media events on campus?
8. Should you give the Biblical perspective on issues even if the humanists don't like it?
9. Should you seek to take over the student government for Christ?
10. Do you bear any social responsibility to the community in which you live?
11. What can you do about the millions of children who are brutally murdered in the name of abortion and mercy killing?
12. Should you be actively involved in demonstrations which support civil rights such as "pro-life" marches?

FIVE

The Christian World View

While you may not be planning to take a course in philosophy while at college, you will actually be studying philosophy in every single class you take. Every professor will be teaching his subject from the perspective of a certain identifiable world view. This means that regardless if you are taking courses in mathematics, nursing, art, psychology, history, social studies or political science, you are in reality being taught somebody's philosophic world view.

What is a world view? When we speak of a "world view," we are talking about the way we interpret all of life. We all try to understand ourselves, the world around us and all the interpersonal relationships that are involved. A world view has to do with the assumptions and the presuppositions which structure our understanding of the universe. Our values and priorities arise out of our world view.

Perhaps one illustration will help at this point. If you put on a pair of pink-tinted glasses, everything you see will be tinted pink. This does not mean that the piece of white paper is actually pink but that it appears pink to you because of the glasses you are wearing. The same can be said of the person who is wearing green-tinted sunglasses. Everything they see around them is tinted green. Your world view can color your perception of the world.

The Christian looks at the world through the glasses of the Bible. These glasses are not tinted but clear and enable the believer to see life as it really is. Humanists have a warped view of reality because they see life through tinted glasses. Their world view keeps them from seeing the world as it really is.

In the Christian world view, man was created by God. Thus when a Christian looks at a man he sees an image-bearer of God who has intrinsic significance, worth and meaning. In humanistic world views, man is a product of meaningless evolution. Thus when a humanist looks at the same man he only sees an animal which has no intrinsic significance, worth or meaning. It does not matter what issue is being discussed, the Christian and the humanist will always have radically different interpretations.

Everyone Is a Philosopher

Even though you may never have thought of yourself as a philosopher, you already have a world view. You may have picked up your world view much like a dog picks up fleas. In other words, you have picked up ideas here and there without any regard for consistency, unity or coherence.

Your present world view is probably the result of the influence of your parents, church, friends and school teachers. Perhaps you are the kind of person that has been deeply influenced by books and movies. Regardless of how or where you got your world view, it is time for you to reflect not only on what you believe but also why you believe it.

How We Get Our World Views

There are three basic ways that a person develops a world view. In the first instance, the person simply accepts the world view that has been taught him. The teaching may be theism from Christian parents or atheism from humanistic parents. Thus while some people believe in God because they were taught to believe in God, others do not believe in God because they were taught not to believe in God. In both cases, the reasons as to why they believe what they believe are never reflected upon. This person, regardless of whether he is a theist or an atheist, is living an unexamined life.

In the second instance, there are those who have decided to take what has been called a "leap in the dark." That is, they choose to believe or not to believe simply on the basis of what they feel or want.

This is indicative of those who have imbibed the bitter waters of existentialism which says there is no meaning, truth or absolutes in the universe. Thus it does not really matter what you believe as long as it makes you feel happy and comfortable.

In other words, something is true if you believe it. Truth in this sense has been totally relativized. It no longer has any objective meaning whatsoever. What is true to you may not be true to me and may not be true to others but it is, nevertheless, true because you believe it. Thus it does not really matter what world view you adopt. You pay your nickel and take your choice because no one has *the* truth.

Some Christians have unknowingly fallen into this existential trap. They assume that Christianity is true because they believe it. They were taught Christianity in their home and in their church and they have always believed it. Therefore they assume that it is true. They do not believe in Christianity because it is true; it is true because they believe it.

In the third instance, someone may adopt a world view because they believe that it is true in an objective and absolute sense. That is, after weighing all the evidences, arguments and implications of different world views, they have decided to adopt that world view which in their mind is really the truth.

They are not concerned if they like this truth or if it makes them feel happy. They are not concerned whether anyone else likes it or accepts it. They will believe something if it is true. If it is not true, they will not believe it regardless of any other considerations.

The Christian Way

Biblical Christianity falls into this third category. The kind of faith spoken of in Scripture is not to be interpreted in an existential sense. God never calls upon us to make a "leap in the dark." Instead He says,

"Come now, and let us reason together, says the Lord."

(Isa. 1:18)

In the book of Acts, we find that the Apostle Paul gave logical arguments from Scripture to demonstrate that Jesus was the Messiah (Acts 19:8). When he dealt with Greek philosophers, he argued for monotheism (Acts 17:16-33). Nowhere did he ask people to take a mindless "leap in the dark" and believe in Jesus because it felt good.

We are asked to believe in the resurrection of Christ because,

"He showed himself to these men and gave many convincing proofs that he was alive."

(Acts 1:3)

People were not asked to believe in the resurrection of Christ simply "by faith." The resurrection of Christ was to be accepted because the evidence for it was so overwhelming that it was not rationally possible to deny it. Thus, Luke in Acts 1:3-4 and Paul in I Cor. 15 give the evidences and the arguments which demonstrate the truthfulness of Christ's resurrection. We are asked to believe that Christ actually arose from the dead because the evidence demonstrates that His resurrection actually happened in real space-time history.

This rugged attitude toward truth is exemplified and honored in Acts 17:10-12.

"As soon as it was night, the brothers sent Paul and Silas away to Berea. On arriving there, they went to the Jewish synagogue. Now the Bereans were of more noble character than the Thessalonians, for they received the message with great eagerness and examined the Scriptures every day to see if what Paul said was true. Many of the Jews believed, as did also a number of prominent Greek women and many Greek men.''

In the passage above, the Bereans were praised because they did not simply accept what Paul had to say on the basis of an existential ''leap in the dark.'' Instead, they searched the Scriptures to see if what Paul was saying was really true. Once they were convinced by the evidence Paul gave that Jesus was indeed the Messiah, they believed in Him. Their faith was based upon the truth and not vice versa.

Where the Confusion Comes In

Some Christian students have been deceived on this point. They have been taught by religious existentialists that Christianity is not based on evidence or proof. One accepts Christ solely on the basis of ''faith.''

These students were encouraged not to ask questions. They were told that philosophy and logic were ''bad.'' They were told that if you look too closely at the Bible, you would discover that there is no evidence to support it. Thus Christianity is something that one accepts pietistically solely on the basis of a ''leap in the dark'' kind of faith. This attitude has driven many intellectuals from the Church.

Biblically based Christians do not accept existentialism in its secular or religious forms because they know that it is self-refuting. When someone tells you, ''There are no absolutes,'' they want you to accept that statement as an absolute! When they tell you, ''There is no truth,'' they want you to accept that statement as the truth! When they say, ''Everything is relative,'' they want you to accept that statement as an absolute! The moment they make such statements they have refuted themselves.

When Thomas demanded proof of the resurrection of Christ, he was not rebuked because he wanted to know if the resurrection really happened. Christ physically demonstrated to him that He had in fact been bodily raised from the dead.

"Now Thomas (called Didymus), one of the Twelve, was not with the disciples when Jesus came. When the other disciples told him that they had seen the Lord, he declared, 'Unless I see the nail marks in his hands and put my finger where the nails were, and put my hand into his side, I will not believe it.'

"A week later his disciples were in the house again, and Thomas was with them. Though the doors were locked, Jesus came and stood among them and said, 'Peace be with you!' Then he said to Thomas, 'Put your finger here; see my hands. Reach out your hand and put it into my side. Stop doubting and believe.'

"Thomas said to him, 'My Lord and my God!' "
(John 20:24-28)

Philosophy and science actually depend on the Bible for their validity because all the laws of logic are based upon the unalterable character of the God who cannot lie (Heb. 6:18). Whenever the Scriptures have been investigated empirically or logically, they have always been vindicated. Christianity should be accepted because it is true.

The Importance of the Bible

The Christian world view is based upon the Bible as the inspired Word of God. When we look into the Bible we find that the authors of Scripture never appeal to human reason, experience or emotion as being the origin, basis, or judge of truth, morals, justice or beauty. The Bible does not point us to man as if man is capable of discovering truth apart from God. It always points us to God as the Origin of Meaning. Man is the receiver of truth and not its creator.

This is why the Bible begins with God and not with man.

It begins at the very beginning and goes right through to the end. All of space-time history is covered in the 66 books of the Bible. From the Creation of the world to the End of the world all of history is mapped out by the Word of God.

In the first book of the Bible, Genesis, in the very first three chapters of that first book, we find the three foundational presuppositions by which all of life is to be interpreted.

The Three Foundational Truths

Genesis chapt. 1-3 unfold the three truths of Creation, Fall and Redemption as being the foundational concepts of biblical religion.

1. Thematically, everything else in Scripture is a development of these three concepts.
2. Exegetically, these three concepts serve as the glasses through which we understand and interpret all of life.
3. When Jesus dealt with the subject of marriage and divorce, He interpreted it in the light of Creation-Fall-Redemption (Matt. 19:1-6).
4. Paul always used Creation-Fall-Redemption as the motif by which all of life could interpreted.
   a. The male and female roles in the home and in the church (I Cor. 11:3-12; I Tim. 2:12-14).
   b. Whether certain foods are to be viewed as intrinsically "evil" and should be avoided by Christians (I Tim. 4:1-5).
   c. Why the world is in a state of chaos and decay and and how the world will one day be returned to perfection (Rom. 8:18-23).

To understand anything from the Christian perspective requires that the subject be looked at from the standpoint of Creation-Fall-Redemption. The failure to take these biblical themes seriously renders any attempt to construct a Christian world view impossible.

I. The Creation

In Gen. 1, we discover that the universe is not eternal. It has a distinct beginning. The only eternal being is God Himself. He has always existed as the eternal "I AM."

God did not create the universe out of any pre-existing materials. He spoke the worlds into existence (Heb. 11:3). By an act of His divine will He brought the universe "out of nothing."

Neither is the universe to be viewed as being made out of the being of God. The universe was not made of any aspect of God's essence or nature. It has its own separate existence apart from the existence of God. Its existence, or being, is qualitatively distinct from the existence of the Creator.

Whereas the universe is finite, temporal and dependent, God is infinite, eternal and independent. The universe relies upon God for its very existence (Col. 1:16-17). God relies on no one and on nothing for His own existence. He is eternal.

From the biblical concept of Creation we learn the following things:

1. *The world was created out of nothing.*

This means that all concepts which involve the eternity of matter or energy are false. There is no such thing as eternal hydrogen molecules. The universe is not in a state of oscillation in which it expands and contracts eternally.

2. *The creation is distinct from the Creator.*

There are two different kinds of existence or being. This means that all concepts of monism, which involves the idea that reality exists only of one kind of being and existence, are erroneous. Pantheism, panentheism and paneverythingism are false concepts.

3. *The material universe exists.*

This means that any philosophy or religion which denies the existence of material reality must be rejected. Be it Buddhism or Christian Science, any denial of physical reality must be rejected. All forms of spiritualism, which reduces reality to immaterial things such as the mind or cosmic energy, are wrong.

4. *The spiritual universe exists.*

God created not only the material universe but immaterial beings such as angels and immaterial things such as the human soul or spirit. This means that materialism which reduces all of reality to material objects must be rejected by Christians.

5. *After God created the universe which has both matter and spirit, He declared that it was "very good"* (Gen. 1:31).

This means that the material world is not to be viewed as evil. The human body is not to be viewed as evil nor any of its functions or purposes. Thus the Christian rejects all philosophic or religious world views that entail the evilness of matter or of the human body.

6. *The universe was not created by accident.*

God has His own plans for the universe and for history itself. Thus we read in such places as Eph. 1:11,

"The plan of Him who works out everything in conformity with the purpose of His will."

Thus everything in life has purpose and meaning from the very beginning (Pro. 16:4; Ecc. 3:1). This stands in contradiction of those views of the universe which would see life as a gamble based on blind luck and contingency. They would view life as having no meaning or purpose. This the Christian cannot accept.

7. *The universe does not begin with the impersonal but with the personal because it begins with the personal Creator.*

Man is not in contradiction of his own existence. His personality is reflective of the personal Creator who made him. This means that all humanistic views which reduce man to the level of an animal or a machine must be viewed as erroneous.

8. *Because man was created in the image of God, we must view man as a unique creature who stands outside of the rest of the Creation.*

Indeed, God placed man over the earth to rule as His vice-regent (Gen. 1:26-29). Man stands outside of the cosmic machine. Any world view which traps man in "nature" is false. Man stands outside of nature as its prophet, priest and king.

He is not an animal or a machine but the unique image bearer of God.

9. *We can speak of the unity and dignity of mankind only because all of humanity ultimately came from Adam and Eve.*

The different races are simply genetic variations on the descendants of Adam and Eve. The unity and dignity of man depend upon the Adam and Eve model of creation. We can speak of "mankind" because we all came from Adam and Eve.

This is in stark contrast to some humanistic ideas of evolution which view each race of man as evolving from different primates. If this is true, then one race could claim to be superior over the other races. Slavery could be justified because there is no such thing as "mankind."

10. *Because man is God's image bearer, he is a responsible moral agent who will be held accountable by God for his thoughts, words and deeds on the Day of Judgment at the end of the world.*

While animals are not viewed in the Bible as responsible moral agents because they do not have immortal souls, man is viewed in this way. This means that all views of man which negate his being responsible for his own actions must be rejected. The Christian view does not accept any chemical, environmental, societal or economical determinism. Man is not the victim of his circumstances. He will be held accountable for what he does.

II. The Fall

The Bible tells us that at the very beginning of human history man fell into a state of sin and guilt. The radical Fall of man is viewed by the biblical authors as being a real event in space-time history (Rom. 5:12ff; I Cor. 15:21ff). It is never viewed as a myth. It was an actual event which you could have witnessed with your own eyes.

The original sin was not sex. It was rebellion against God and His Law. Man attempted to become his own god (Gen.

3:5). Self-deification is one way in which man tries to be autonomous, i.e., independent from God. This is always the goal of apostate thought. Indeed, the history of philosophy is nothing more than man's attempt to escape God and His Law.

In his temptation, Satan told man three lies:

1. You can be whatever you want to be.

This lie denies that man is a finite being and is thus limited by his finite nature. Just as man is not a bird and thus he cannot flap his arms and fly away, neither is he autonomous. We can be only what God has made us to be.

2. You can know whatever you want to know.

This denies that man's understanding is finite. But man and his thoughts are finite and, hence, cannot obtain an infinite comprehension of anything. We can know only what God has made us capable of knowing.

3. You can do whatever you want to do.

In this lie man is told that he can be his own law-giver. He does not have to obey God's Law but he can make up his own laws. Unbelief comes man's rebellion against God and His Law.

The biblical account of man's radical fall into sin gives us a key to understanding life. The world that now exists is not to be viewed as "normal." This means that death is not normal. Sin is not normal. Evil is not normal. Man is now subnormal. His problem is not his humanity but his depravity. Man's problem is not that he is finite but that he is a sinner by nature (Eph. 2:1-3).

The old saying, "To err is human but to forgive is divine," is built on the humanistic assumption that man's problem is his humanity. But this is not true. Adam and Eve were created righteous in the beginning. They were human and sinless at the same time. Jesus Christ was a real human being but He was also sinless. After the Resurrection, believers will be sinless. "Humanness" does not automatically mean sinfulness.

Once you equate "humanness" with sinfulness, you arrive at the basis of the liberal denial of the inspiration of Scripture. They usually argue in this way,

"Since 'to err is human,' and the Bible was written by humans, this means that the Bible has to have errors. The errors and contradictions in the Bible only prove its humanness."

This argument fails to take into account man's original righteousness, his subsequent Fall into sin and guilt and the sinlessness of Jesus Christ (II Cor. 5:21). The Living Word and the Written Word are both errorless and sinless. Man's problems are fundamentally *moral* in nature and not physical, environmental or social.

III. Redemption

According to Scripture, God did not leave man in a state of sin and guilt. As we demonstrated in *The Saving Work of Christ,* the triune God of Father, Son and Holy Spirit worked together to provide a salvation for sinners.

God the Father planned salvation from eternity past (Eph. 1:4). God the Son entered history and died on the cross for the sins of His people (I Cor. 15:3, 4). And God the Holy Spirit takes what Christ accomplished according to the plan of the Father and applies it to the people of God (Eph. 4:30).

"We are chosen by the Father, purchased by the Son, sealed by the Spirit, blessed God Three in One."

God's wondrous plan of Redemption began in eternity past and secures eternity future for His people. Jesus Christ has entered history and through His life, death and resurrection has created a new humanity which will one day enjoy a new earth which has been returned to its original paradise condition (II Pet. 3:11-13).

Summary

The biblical world view of Creation-Fall-Redemption supplies us with the only way of understanding reality as it really is. If we do not accept the biblical world view, we will never find truth, justice, morals or beauty.

Questions for Discussion

1. What is a world view?
2. Where did you get your world view?
3. Have you ever thought about why you believe what you believe?
4. Is something true simply because you believe it?
5. Is Christianity a "leap into the dark" or are there good evidences which back up the Bible and its claims?
6. What is existentialism?
7. What are the three foundational concepts of the Bible?
8. What ten facts arise from Creation-Fall-Redemption?
9. If we do not start with the biblical world view, is it possible to understand life?
10. What logical implications does the theory of evolution have on the subject of racism?

SIX

Five Great Facts

There are five great facts of reality which must be explained by any world view. The degree to which a world view recognizes and gives satisfying answers to these five facts determines its validity.

Fact #1: *The existence of the universe.*

The fact of the existence of the universe of men and things cannot be ignored. While it can be denied, it cannot be escaped. The same Hindu who denies the reality of the material universe must eat and drink like everyone else. While he may deny that his material body exists, he cannot escape the reality of having to clothe and feed it. In other words, he cannot live what he believes!

A world view must recognize and explain why the universe exists rather than not existing.

Fact #2: *The form of the universe.*

The universe that confronts us is not formless or lawless. It is not a willy-nilly universe where each of us experiences his own private reality. If a Jew, a Christian, a Muslim, a Hindu, an atheist, and a Buddhist jump off the same cliff, they will all die because the universe that exists is one in which there is a law of gravity which does not care what you may or may not believe. Someone may claim that the universe is devoid of law but they still have to obey the laws. They cannot live what they believe.

A world view must recognize and explain why the form

of the universe is what it is rather than being formless.

Fact #3: *The uniqueness of man.*

Man cannot be reduced to a rock or to an animal. His desire to find truth, justice, morals, meaning and beauty immediately sets him apart from the rest of creation. He is unique in so many ways. He is a cognitive ego who can say, "I am." He can make and appreciate art. He cannot escape giving moral judgments. The "manishness" of man is something that cannot be ignored or escaped.

A world view must recognize and explain why man is unique.

Fact #4: *The failure of humanism.*

Humanists have tried for thousands of years to explain man and the world around him on the sole basis of reason, emotions and experience. But the reality which confronts us all is that rationalism, mysticism and empiricism have never been able to generate a sufficient basis for truth, justice, morals, meaning or beauty. After all is said and done, when man attempts to "go it alone," he fails to get anywhere.

What has humanistic thought produced after thousands of years? It has produced *Skepticism* which denies that there are any truths to find, *Relativism* which denies there are any morals by which you can judge right from wrong, and *Existentialism* which denies that life has any meaning at all. As a world view humanism has failed to recognize or explain the existence and form of the universe, the uniqueness of man, and its own failure.

One illustration of how humanism has failed would be its attempt to find meaning without God. As we pointed out in the *Battle of the Gods* (Crowne Pub.), the Greek philosopher Plato tried to find meaning for the things around him by stating that the meaning of something was not to be found "down here," but was to be found "up there" in the World of Ideas. Thus while a thing did not have meaning in and of itself, the idea of the thing is what has meaning.

If you pointed to a dog, Plato would say that the dog in front of you did not have any meaning in and of itself. But the idea of "dogness" is what gives meaning to the dog in front of you. The dog had meaning only because there was the idea of dogness in the World of Ideas.

When Aristotle came along he saw that Plato had not really given any "meaning" to the dog but he had simply duplicated him in the World of Ideas. In other words, the idea of dogness also needed to have "meaning." To shuffle the dog from this world "down here" to another world "up there" did not solve anything.

Aristotle thought he could solve the problem by dumping the concept of a "World of Ideas." Instead, he taught that meaning could be found "in" the thing itself. It is possible to abstract or discern the "essence" or "meaning" that exists in objects. Thus as you examine the dog, you will find that the object has its own intrinsic meaning and all you have to do is to abstract the essence or meaning of it. Meaning is not "up there" but "down here."

Although other variations to Aristotle's themes have been developed during the Middle Ages, particularly by Thomas Aquinas, when we arrive at the Renaissance and, in particular, the so-called "Age of Enlightenment," we arrive at the correspondence theory of meaning.

This theory stated that objects have meaning within themselves if there is a corresponding meaning in the mind of man. Thus meaning is "out there" in the object and "in here" in the mind of man.

One such philosopher who taught this was Leibnez. He stated that the meaning must be in the mind as well as in the object and when the two meanings contact, knowledge takes place.

The next stage of development in humanistic thinking was Emmanual Kant. He is so important that the history of philosophy is divided into pre-Kantian and post-Kantian philosophy.

Kant's claim to fame was to deny that there was any meaning in Plato's World of Ideas, in Aristotle's thing in itself, or in the correspondence between the mind and the object as in

Liebnez. Instead, Kant proposed that all meaning is to be found in the mind of man. This means that objects or the thing in itself has no meaning except what the human mind projects on to it.

Kant's epistemology involves the ability of the human mind to project order and meaning onto life through the categories of the mind. Thus meaning was not "up there," "down here," or "out there" but only "in here" in the mind of man! The humanists were running out of options.

Humanistic philosophy was now ready to shift from essentialism, which had assumed that objects had an "essence" or "meaning," to existentialism, which stated that things exist without having any "essence" or "meaning."

If meaning was not to be found in Plato's World of Ideas, Aristotle's essence and form, in Leibnez's correspondence theory, or in Kant's categories of the mind, the existentialists such as Sartre concluded that meaning cannot be found anywhere. Nothing including man has any real meaning. Meaning was not "up there," "down here," "out there," or "in here." It was nowhere.

Sartre went further than to simply deny the existence of meaning. He pointed out that a particular must have an infinite reference point in order to have any meaning whatsoever. This infinite reference point could only be found in the infinite God of the Scriptures. Happily, toward the end of his life, Sartre abandoned existentialism and returned to belief in God as the only hope of man.

This is the modern humanistic problem. God is no longer acceptable to modern humanists. In this sense, God is dead to them. Since they cannot accept God, they find themselves without a sufficient basis for meaning, hope, significance, love, truth, morals or justice.

Once we reject the God who is the infinite reference point and thus is the Origin of Meaning, then we must reject everything that flows from that God such as the dignity and worth of man and that life has any significance or meaning. In other words, if God is dead then man is dead. And if man is dead then truth, justice, morality and beauty are likewise dead.

The present philosophy of death and despair that grips the secular campus is self-refuting. When a humanist says, "There is no meaning," the statement is self-refuting because he wants you to grasp the *meaning* of this statement. When he says, "There is no truth," he wants you to accept that statement as *true!* He is cutting his own throat when he makes such stupid statements.

A world view must explain why humanism has failed to find a sufficient basis for truth, justice, morality, meaning and beauty.

Fact #5: *The superiority of the Christian world view.*

The Bible gives us a satisfying explanation of the existence and form of the universe, the uniqueness of man and the failure of humanism. When man attempts to understand the world without God's special revelation given in Scripture he always ends in foolishness (I Cor. 1:20-25; Rom. 1:21-23). Only the Bible gives us a sufficient basis for truth, justice, morals, meaning and beauty.

Summary

Man has failed to escape the necessity of divine Revelation. He cannot know anything as it really is if he does not begin with God as He has revealed Himself in the Bible.

The God who has revealed Himself in Scripture is the infinite reference point which supplies us with the absolutes we need to distinguish reality from fantasy, truth from falsehood, justice from injustice, good from evil, right from wrong and ugliness from beauty.

Questions for Discussion

1. What five great facts have to be explained?

2. Humanism has led to skepticism and relativism. What do these words mean?
3. How has humanistic philosophy tried to find meaning?
4. What is the only way for man to have meaning and significance?
5. How is the Christian world view better than humanism?

SEVEN

Christianity and Culture

There are ten basic principles which reveal why humanism is now the dominant force in the United States. These ten principles must be grasped by Christians in order for them to understand why humanism has gained the upper hand.

1. A person's beliefs, values and morals will always be reflected in the way that person lives. His life style will reflect his beliefs.

This law of life is taught in the Scriptures in such places as Pro. 23:7 and Matt. 12:33-37. Those who believe that they are only animals will generally live like one. Those who believe that they are the children of God and are called upon by God to take dominion over the earth will live in accordance with that idea.

2. The Scriptures command us to judge people on the basis of how they live.

When Jesus said in Matt. 7:1, "Judge not lest you be judged," He was referring to the hypocrisy of the Pharisees who condemned people for doing certain sins that they themselves were actually doing (Matt. 7:5). When Jesus was speaking to His own disciples He told them to "judge righteous judgement" (John 7:24). We are called upon in Scripture to identify and to reject false prophets (Deut. 18:21, 22; Matt. 7:15-23). Paul warns us concerning those who would claim to be Christians but their lifestyle refutes that claim (Gal. 5:19-21). John tells us to identify people who live in disobedience to God's Word as "liars" if they claim to be Christians (I John 2:4).

3. The culture of a nation reflects the life style of those who are involved in the culture-forming process.

The philosophers, artists, teachers, politicians, lawyers, judges, doctors, wealthy people, the clergy, media people, etc., will lead a nation either into wickedness or righteousness. The cutting edge of a culture always sets the standard for morality and justice. This cutting edge is generally composed of the professional people of that society. Their influence far exceeds their numbers.

4. We have the biblical responsibility to judge a culture on the basis of its laws because these laws are simply codified life styles.

It was on this basis that the Egyptian, Canaanite and Philistine cultures were judged worthy of destruction. Paul could condemn the Cretian culture as decadent (Tit. 1:10-13). We can condemn such modern cultures as Hitler's Third Reich or the Soviet Union.

The concept of cultural relativism in which all cultures are to be viewed as good is condemned by Scripture. The people who usually teach the idea of cultural relativism are hypocrites because they also teach that Western or American culture is decadent and evil. They never seem to realize the contradiction between the two ideas. If all cultures are good, then how can they condemn American culture? How can they condemn Christian missionaries for spreading their culture in the Third World? Isn't their culture good?

5. Pre-Christian, Greek, and Roman pagan cultures codified laws supporting abortion, infanticide, child abuse, rape, suicide, incest, murder for entertainment, etc., because these things were a part of their life style.

6. When enough Christians became involved in the culture forming process of the Roman Empire, they became the cutting edge of that culture. Their beliefs, values and morals led them to repeal pagan laws and to legislate biblical laws. Thus the state ended up forbidding the very things which the pre-

vious pagan culture had honored.

7. Western history, in term of its culture, was basically Christian because its laws reflected the beliefs, values and morals of the Scriptures.

Even to this day, there are many laws still on the books which reflect biblical morality. Those people who say, "You cannot legislate morality," are absurd. Every law ever legislated was instituting somebody's morality.

8. Christians in the United States during the 1920's fell into a pietistic focus on one's personal devotion to Christ that led them to abandon the culture-forming process.

It was assumed that it would be unspiritual for Christians to be involved in law, medicine, education, entertainment, government, art, etc. Their only concern was "soul winning." This led them to abandon any attempt to influence their society for the good. This extreme separationism was in clear violation of Paul's explicit statements in I Cor. 5:9-13.

9. Because Christians abandoned the culture-forming process, a vacuum was created in the United States and the humanists moved into this vacuum.

Instead of there being Christian lawyers, judges, politicians, teachers, artists, etc., Christians were only involved in evangelism or missions. The idea of "full time Christian service" meant only the clergy or missionary profession.

The vacuum created by the retreat of the Christians was filled by the humanists. Since they were now in control of the government, public education and the media, they have begun to reinstate the laws which reflect their pagan life style. This is why the laws are changing on such issues as abortion, infanticide, mercy killing, etc. Modern humanists are putting into law what they believe.

The historic understanding of the Constitution and the Bill of Rights is now being overthrown. Modern humanists do not believe in the historic meaning of the freedom of religion. If the humanists have their way, the freedom of religion will be limited to believing what you want but not the freedom to practice it!

As we document in *The New Atheism and the Erosion of Freedom,* modern humanists do not believe that Christians have the "freedom" to teach their religion to their children, witness, pass out tracts or show any public signs of religion. The only "freedom" they will allow is freedom *from* religion.

Modern laws which legalize such things as abortion come from humanists who are legislating their view of morality. They are legalizing their pagan life style while trying to criminalize Christian education, church camps and orphanages, personal evangelism, Christian TV and radio programs, etc. Their understanding of religious freedom is the same as found in the Soviet Union!

10. The only hope for Western culture is for Christians once again to take over the culture-forming process. Then when they are in control, to repeal the pagan laws and to reinstitute Christian laws. If they do not do this, modern pagans will soon be in a position to begin the same kind of persecution against the Church that their forefathers in the Roman Empire had done to the Christians earlier.

Since it took a full generation for Christians to lose control of the culture, it will probably take another generation to win it back. So, do not be fooled by those who look for easy answers and a "quick fix." It won't work! If God does not send us another mighty Reformation, Western culture will die.

Summary

Those of you who are students will have to be the generation that takes over our culture by becoming politicians, media people, artists, lawyers and judges. The survival of Western civilization falls on your shoulders. Only you can gain control of our culture and once again institute biblical laws which make up a just and orderly society.

Questions for Discussion

1. How is a culture formed?
2. How did our culture become so pagan?
3. Who allowed the humanists to take over?
4. What is the "cutting edge" of a culture?
5. Where do laws come from?
6. Can you legislate morality or immorality?

EIGHT

Humanism and Human Life

Humanism teaches that man is the result of a chance-governed evolutionary process in a closed system wherein God or any act of God is excluded in principle. God is not so much refuted as He is defined out of existence. Since there is no infinite reference point which could possibly give meaning or significance to any particular, human life has no intrinsic value, dignity, freedom or meaning.

While human life or animal life in general has no intrinsic value or dignity, it can have "acquired worth" in terms of its utility or function. When a person's utilitarian worth is over so far as society is concerned, that person no longer has any "right to life."

The "privilege of life" can be withdrawn by the state at will. Because human life has no intrinsic worth, it is perfectly proper, if deemed for purposes of utility, to abort unborn babies, murder babies already born, to put to death those who are sick, handicapped, disabled or old.

The following points are usually argued by humanists to demonstrate that it is perfectly proper to do away with human beings if it is deemed "useful" to society.

1. Economic considerations may lead to the termination of "useless" lives.

This "useless" person may be the child of a welfare mother. It is cheaper to kill that child than to give additional financial aid for the care and raising of that child. Thus it is no wonder that the primary object of the abortion clinic is the killing of black babies rather than giving black women the support they need to raise a family in dignity.

2. People who are "miserable" may be terminated.

The argument is usually given that this person has in their future a "miserable life" due to the fact that they are handicapped or that they may possibly experience pain in the future.

What this argument really means is that those around them will feel "miserable" when they have to care for or look at the individual. Thus physical deformity as well as disability is usually looked upon as viable grounds for abortion or mercy killing.

3. Children who are "unwanted" can be killed.

This killing may take place before they are born which is abortion or after they are born which is infanticide. Pagan judges have upheld both forms of murder.

4. Inconvenient pregnancies can be terminated at will.

Human life has no intrinsic worth and if this child will be inconvenient because it will interfere with your career or personal pleasure, then it is perfectly proper to kill that baby.

5. The "right to life" is not absolute.

There are no inalienable rights given by a divine Creator to anyone because there is no God. Rights are given by the state and can be withdrawn by the state at will.

6. Over-population necessitates the killing of worthless human beings.

This means that the unwanted, the handicapped, the terminally ill, or the elderly should be encouraged to take their own life or they should be forced into suicide clinics where their life will be forcibly taken from them. Death pills or suicide pills should be made available to anyone who wishes to take his life.

7. In the future there will be food and fuel shortages which means that the state will have to "liquidate" unnecessary "assets," i.e., people.

8. The few (i.e., the poor, the sick and the elderly) should

be willing to sacrifice for the many (i.e., the wealthy, healthy and young).

They should be willing to go to suicide clinics so the rest of us can enjoy life.

9. If someone wants to die, doctors should be willing to perform this task. Physicians should become doctors of death as they did in the Third Reich.

10. People who can no longer make any contribution to society are to be viewed as "parasites" and since they do not produce any goods or services, they should be "terminated."

This is what communist countries have practiced for years. Life is cheap where there is no God.

Summary

Without God, human life loses all dignity and worth. Man is reduced to an animal and is treated as such.

Questions for Discussion

1. What do you think of the argument that if a baby is not wanted and he would be inconvenient, it is all right to kill that baby?
2. Should your grandparents be put to death because they are old?
3. If someone asks to die, is it all right to kill them?
4. Have you ever felt you wanted to die? What if some doctor decided to kill you at that time? Would it be all right?
5. Your brother is mentally retarded and lives at home with you. What would you do if the government decided he should be terminated?
6. You have been told that you are not allowed to have children because your IQ is not high enough. How would you respond?
7. Should governments force abortions on people?

NINE

Christianity and Human Life

Man was created in the image of God. Thus every human being from the moment of conception to death has intrinsic worth and inalienable rights. The intrinsic worth and dignity of man is immutable and cannot be affected by a lack of "acquired worth" or "economic considerations." The utility of a person has no bearing whatsoever on the issue of the worth of man as the image bearer of God.

The sanctity of human life is clearly taught in Scripture. The killing of human beings because they are in the way of personal pleasure or affluence is murder. Only the God who gave life has the right to order the death of anyone. This is why Christians believe in capital punishment and are against abortion at the same time. While God has ordered capital punishment in certain cases (Gen. 9:6), He has condemned the killing of the innocent (Exo. 20:13).

The Sanctity of Life Declaration

1. Genetic experimentation on fertilized human eggs is morally wrong and should be illegal because the destruction of such eggs is the killing of human life. Some techniques used to overcome infertility are immoral and should be made illegal. When fertilized human eggs are washed down the sink, this is the murder of innocent human beings.

101

2. It is morally wrong and should be illegal to experiment on the human DNA code to predetermine the race, sex or physical characteristics of human beings. Human beings should not be genetically programmed or "bred" as is done with cattle. We have already seen how Hitler's dream of breeding a "super-race" ended.

3. Abortion is morally wrong and should be made illegal except where the life of the mother is threatened. Even though the case where the life of a mother is threatened is exceedingly rare, yet the biblical principle would be to preserve the life of the mother as opposed to the life of the child.

4. All acts of infanticide in which babies are murdered either through active or passive means are immoral and should be made illegal regardless of what economic or other considerations are made.

Active means of infanticide include choking the child to death, stabbing the child in the heart or poisoning the child. Passive usually means placing the child in a closet or in a container and allowing the child to die slowly and excruciatingly through starvation and dehydration. Some have cried for days before they died a horrible death. If someone killed a dog this way, it would be viewed as a crime. How then can human babies be killed this way without criminal charges? Have we come to the place where to kill a dog is more heinous than the murder of precious little babies?

5. All so-called "mercy killing" is morally wrong and should remain illegal. It is nothing more than murder regardless if it is done through passive or active means.

6. Active or passive euthanasia is morally wrong and should be made illegal. To encourage the elderly to commit suicide is to aid and abet murder.

7. Medical care should not involve age limits or "useful life" standards. To deny medical care to someone because they are no longer viewed as being "useful" is nothing but murder.

8. Suicide should not be legalized. Suicide clinics or "death pills" should not be forced on or offered to the elderly.

9. The state should not have any "final solution" for

"undesirables." This is exactly what Hitler did to Jews, gypsies and other ethnic and racial groups which they deemed as "undesirables."

10. There should be no program of "liquidation" of those who think or teach differently than the state.

The Gulags of the Soviet Union and the gas chambers of the Nazis both resulted in death for anyone who thought or taught differently than state policy. This is immoral and should remain illegal.

Summary

The end result of humanism is death while Christianity brings life and light through the Gospel. Humanism brings man down to the level of an animal while Christianity lifts him up to be the image bearer of God. Christians are the only ones on campus who promote life. The humanists are the merchants of death.

Questions for Discussion

1. How do humanists view human life?
2. How do Christians view human life?
3. What do you think about abortion, infanticide, mercy killing and euthanasia?
4. Explain: "Christians believe in life."
5. What will happen to our culture if Christians do not regain control?
6. Is genetic engineering moral?
7. What countries have put a humanistic view of man into practice?

TEN

Do Not Be Deceived

We know that it is difficult for young people to accept the fact that there are religious groups which knowingly use lies and deception to convert people. It can come as quite a shock to some people that not all religious people are sincere and that some religions are no more than glorified con games run to make the leaders rich.

The typical Christian student was raised in a sincere religious home, attended a church which was honest and went through a Christian school system which valued truth and morals. Then he comes to a college where he meets new religions. He naturally assumes that they must be as sincere as were his parents and pastor. But this is a deadly mistake.

Most of the cultic groups which are recruiting students on today's campus only want three things out of their recruits: their money, their mind and body. In order to get these things, they will lie, cheat, and steal. They will use sex and drugs. They will use the same brainwashing techniques used by the Communists. A congressional subcommittee found that some cults put people under hypnotic control and that they will kill people if the need arises.

All of this means that religion is not the innocent game that most people think it is. People have died as a result of such cults as Christian Science, Jehovah's Witnesses, the People's Temple, Hare Krishnas, Black Muslims and many others. If you fail to heed the warning of Jesus, you might lose your life as well as your immortal soul.

Just because some group, church or organization says it is "Christian" does not mean that it is Christian. Just because someone tells you that he believes in "God" or "Jesus" does not mean that he believes in the same God or Jesus you do.

You probably will meet some people who say, "All religions are the same because they all worship the same God under different names. So, it does not really matter what religion you believe as long as it makes you happy."

Such statements are totally irrational. Logically speaking, since all religions contradict each other, either one of them is true and the others false or they are all false. They cannot all be true.

Words can have different meanings. Such words as God, Christ, Jesus and salvation are redefined by the cults and given a meaning that is anti-Christian. For example, when a Christian uses the word "God" he is referring to the only true God of Father, Son and Holy Spirit who is infinite in His nature and thus eternal, omnipresent, omniscient, omnipotent and sovereign. But when a Mormon uses the word "God" he is referring to one of many finite gods who were men and women at one time and have now become deities. Obviously there is no relationship between the Christian concept of God and Mormon theology. See the *Battle of the Gods* for further details.

When people ask you, "Is Christianity the one true religion?" go ahead and sweetly tell them, "Yes! And thank God it is or there would be no salvation." They will often argue that your belief is wrong because "Truth is whatever we want it to be." Point out to them that they are being hypocritical at this point for they are claiming that their view is "true" and yours is "wrong!" It never fails to amaze us when people say that all religions are true but then turn right around and say that Christianity is wrong! They cannot have their cake and eat it too!

The same kind hypocrisy is found in people who argue, "It is not right to push your views on others." They will even condemn you for witnessing to them. The only problem is that *they* are trying to push their views on you! Do not let them get away with it.

All religions do not worship the same God. Obviously, it would be totally irrational to claim that monotheism is the same as polytheism. The same can be said of the Eastern cults such as Hinduism or Zen Buddhism which would define the entire universe as God. Pantheism cannot be reconciled with the personal God of the Bible.

Some humanists will challenge you by asking,

"But what about the heathen? Do you mean to tell me that they are going to hell just because they never heard of your Jesus?"

There is no reason for Christians to feel intimidated by this issue. Did Jesus say that He was the ONLY way, the truth, the life and that no one can come to the Father except through Him (John 14:6)? He was either telling the truth or He was lying. Which was it? Did Peter say that Jesus is the ONLY way under heaven to be saved (Acts 4:12)? Was he lying? Can anyone deny that Paul taught that the gospel is the ONLY way of salvation (Rom. 10:9-15)?

All religions claim to be the true religion. A Muslim is a Muslim because he thinks it is the true religion. So, why pick on Christians as if they are the only ones who claim to have the truth. Even the humanists think they're right!

Get the Facts Straight

To answer the heathen question we must get our facts straight.

1. No one goes to hell because he did not hear the gospel. People go to hell because they are sinners who have rebelled against God's Law (Rom. 1:18-32; 2:12-16).

2. No one goes to hell because he rejected the gospel. We were perishing in our sins and under God's condemnation

before we ever heard it (I Cor. 1:18; John 3:36).

3. All of humanity is in a state of sin and guilt and is under the wrath of God (Rom. 3:23). God does not owe salvation to anyone (Rom. 4:1-5). He would be perfectly just if He let everyone go to hell for their sins. It is only by His grace and mercy that anyone is saved.

4. The religions of the world are not the result of man's search for God but man's running from God (Rom. 3:11). People made up false gods and false religions to escape from the Creator (Rom. 1: 18-25). Their worship does not go to God but to the demons (I Cor. 10:20). All the nations that forgot God will be thrown into hell (Psa. 9:17).

One nice way to reply to the question "What about the heathen?" is to ask,

> "Well, what about *you?* Are not *you* one heathen who has heard! I don't think you are really concerned about the heathen. For example, how much money have you given to missions lately? Your question is just your way of trying to escape from your responsibility to repent and to believe the gospel."

But what do you say to people who claim to be Christians but who say that it is not nice to "put down" other religions? They are disregarding Scripture. Jesus did not hesitate to "put down" false religions. He was not afraid to offend religious leaders by telling them that they were not only wrong but hypocrites (Matt. 23). They have to make up their minds if they really want to be Christians. If they do, then they must follow Christ.

God commands us to demolish all the arguments raised against Him (II Cor. 10:4, 5). We are to give logical answers when challenged (I Pet. 3:15). We must defend the faith (Jude 3). Could anything be clearer?

Now, we are not talking about quarreling and shouting or being argumentative. The servant of the Lord must not get involved in such stupid things (II Tim. 2:24). Both Jesus (Matt. 7:6) and Solomon (Pro. 26:4) warn us not to argue with fools.

But we are to be patient and to teach people the truth praying that God will give them repentance (II Tim. 2:25-26).

Summary

Christians are commanded in Scripture to defend the cause of God and truth. The world needs to hear an authoritative gospel. There can be no compromise with sin or false teaching. We are not called to be wimps but bold soldiers engaged in a spiritual warfare with the powers of darkness (Eph. 6:10-18).

Questions for Discussion

1. Are all religions the same? How would you respond to someone who believes that they are?
2. Do all religions worship the same God just under different names?
3. What is the difference between monotheism, polytheism, and pantheism?
4. Did Jesus tell the truth when He said that He was the ONLY way to God?
5. What is the best way to answer the heathen question?
6. Did pagan religions come from man's search for God?
7. How are people hypocritical when they condemn Christians for condemning other religions?
8. Does God expect us to defend the Gospel?

ELEVEN

Signs of a Cult

O ne hundred years ago there were only around a dozen cults with two or three thousand followers. Today there are over 5000 cults operating in the United States alone. A new cult is incorporated every day of the week. No one individual is capable of keeping track of them all.

There has been a cultic explosion in which 60 to 80 million people in the United States are involved in the cults or occult to some degree. And most of these groups focus on converting college students!

Part of Christian maturity is discerning between truth and error (Heb. 5:12-14). This particularly concerns the ability to spot a false prophet (Matt. 7:15-23).

Even if someone says that he believes in the gospel of Jesus and the Holy Spirit, you cannot assume that what he means by such terms is what you mean by such terms. He may have totally different definition of who Jesus was and what the gospel is all about. What "Jesus" does he believe in? The Jesus of the Jehovah's Witnesses whom they claim was only an angel named Michael? The Jesus of the Unitarians who was only a Jewish rabbi? Or, was Jesus God the Son, second person of the Holy Trinity? Paul warns us that,

"I am afraid that just as Eve was deceived by the serpent's cunning, your minds may somehow be led astray from your sincere and pure devotion to Christ. For if someone comes to you and preaches another

> Jesus other than the Jesus we preached, or if you receive another spirit from the one you received, or another gospel from the one you accepted, you put up with it easily enough."

> (II Cor. 11:3, 4)

The apostle Paul had to deal with false prophets in his own day. They were trying to teach Christian people "another gospel" which was not the true Gospel of Christ. The "Jesus" they preached was not the true Jesus. The "spirit" which animated them was not the Holy Spirit as they claimed but the spirit of antichrist. This is what he said about them:

> "But even if we or an angel from heaven should preach a gospel other than the one we preached to you, let him be eternally condemned! As we have already said, so now I say again: If anybody is preaching to you a gospel other than what you accepted, let him be eternally condemned!"

> (Gal. 1:8, 9)

Paul's Christianity was strong and virile and not wishy-washy. We need to be bold with the truth. It does not matter if someone claims an angel or God Himself appeared and revealed to them a new gospel. Let them be condemned as heretics! Throughout the centuries, false prophets have always come to deceive and confuse the people of God (Deut. 18:21, 22). The Scriptures tell us that we must not be ignorant of Satan's devices (II Cor. 2:11).

In Jude 3, Christians are called upon to defend the Faith. This text also says that the Faith was once and for all delivered unto the saints in the First Century within the pages of the New Testament. This means that the Christian is not to expect or accept any further revelation of doctrines or morals in the future. Thus, the *Book of Mormon* or any other supposed additional revelation which challenge the sole authority of Scripture must be rejected. If a doctrine is not a part of the original historic faith of the Christian Church, it is to be rejected.

What Is a cult?

These considerations help us to define the word "cult." What is a cult?

> "A religion whose leadership is viewed as having equal or greater authority than the Bible and who claims to be Christian while denying the historic doctrines of Biblical Christianity."

The two key issues in the above definition are religious authority and theology. The authority structure of a cult always rests on an infallible leadership who is viewed as being either God's representative or prophet on earth or as God or Christ Himself. Thus the members of the cult must give absolute submission to the authority of the cult leadership. Every aspect of life must be placed in total obedience to the cult. You may not question or challenge the teachings or rulings of the leadership. There is total control of the mind as well as the body in cultic structures.

There are some "Christian" cults operating on campuses today that while they do not deny the fundmental doctrines of the gospel, they are a cult because of their authority structure.

Beware of any group that is against thinking, asking questions, reading books or doing research. When a group emphasizes absolute submission to the leadership, it is cultic in structure.

Most cults deny the theology of Biblical and historic Christianity. The following doctrines are usually the most frequently denied truths.

Signs of a Cult

1. *The Personhood of God*
Most New Age, Eastern or "science of the mind" cults teach that God is an impersonal force or energy. They are not

accountable to a personal God who will one day judge them. It is fruitless to pray for there is no personal God who can hear and answer your prayers. Pantheism is a form of atheism because it denies the biblical God who exists apart from and independent of the universe.

2. *The Trinity*

Most cults deny the doctrine that God eternally exists in the three Persons: the Father, the Son and the Holy Spirit. They either deny that the Son and the Holy Spirit are God or they teach that the Father and the Holy Spirit are only different modes or masks worn by the Son of God who alone is God.

3. *The Virgin Birth*

The cults usually deny that Mary was a virgin when she conceived Jesus. They deny it despite the clear teaching of the Bible in Isa. 7:14; Matt. 1:21-25 and Lk. 1:26-35.

4. *Jesus is the Christ*

All of the New Age, Eastern and "science of the mind" cults believe that the "Christ" is an idea or an ideal which exists in everyone. In this sense, Jesus was only "a" Christ and not THE Christ. Jesus became a Christ at his baptism and ceased to be Christ at his death. There have been many different Christs and you are a Christ too. This is flatly contradicted by the apostle John in I John 2:22.

5. *The bodily resurrection of Christ*

Just as the deity of Christ is rejected by most cults, His bodily resurrection from the dead is also denied. Either His body dissolved into gases as was taught by the early Jehovah's Witnesses or He went on to be reincarnated in other human beings as taught by New Age cults.

6. *The literal return of Christ*

Christians believe that Jesus Christ is going to return to this world with great power and glory and that this return will be personal, bodily and literal. Cultic groups which teach anything concerning the second coming of Christ usually state that the coming was invisible and has already taken place as with the Jehovah's Witnesses. They claim that Jesus returned in

1914. Others claim that Jesus has returned in the person of some present cultic leader as in the New Age Movement.

7. *The atonement of Christ*

The cults always reject the atoning work of Christ in which He dies for the sins of His people and does all that is necessary for their eternal salvation. They speak of atonement only in terms of Jesus being an example of self-giving love. In the science of mind cults, "at-one-ment" means that we are to be absorbed back into the impersonal force of the universe in the classic Hindu sense of Nirvana. Reincarnation is a flat denial of the atonement in that we have to pay off our own karma in some future life.

8. *Justification by grace*

In all cultic structures salvation is based on works. You have to work exceedingly hard at earning your salvation whatever it may be. You may have to go door to door selling magazines, books, flowers or candy in order to fulfill your obligation to the cult. You may have to work day and night in order to deliver your own soul. Baptism is usually made a part of salvation. Eph. 2:8, 9 demonstrates the vanity of trying to work for your salvation.

9. *The authority of Scripture*

One of the most important elements in any cultic structure is that the leadership of the cult has more authority than Scripture itself. Thus the cult member is not under the authority of God or His Word but under the authority of the cult leadership. This is usually hidden from outsiders. They will claim that they believe in the authority of the Bible in order to get you into their meetings. But once you are there, you will discover that the Bible has authority only so far as it agrees with the teachings of the cult.

10. *The new birth*

The cults redefine the new birth as having reference to resurrection as with Armstrong's Worldwide Church of God or reincarnation as with Edgar Casey. They do not accept the teaching of Jesus that we must be born by God's Spirit in order to enter God's kingdom.

11. *Heaven or hell at death*

The cults deny that there is conscious life after death in which the wicked suffer punishment and the righteousness experience bliss in heaven with Christ. They either teach the idea that one is totally unconscious after death or they teach reincarnation in which your soul immediately goes into another infant to start a human life all over again. Christians believe that they go to heaven at death to be with Christ while the wicked go to hell. For a modern defense of the Christian position, see *Death and the Afterlife.*

12. *The Resurrection and Judgment Day*

Many of the cults deny the bodily resurrection of all men at the Day of Judgment. They do not like the idea that they are going to be held accountable by God for how they lived.

13. *The eternal state of the wicked and righteous*

One way to identify someone who is involved in cultic teaching or who is a member of a cultic group is to ask him if he believes in eternal conscious punishment. If he does not believe that the wicked go "into eternal punishment" (Matt. 25:46), then you are dealing with someone who is probably a member of some cultic group.

The same with the eternal blessings of the righteous. We are not going to be continuously recycled like old beer cans. We will dwell with the Lord Jesus on a new earth.

How to Handle Them

What is the most effective way of dealing with cultists? The first thing you must avoid is arguing over peripheral issues. Do not waste your time arguing with Jehovah's Witnesses over saluting the flag or blood transfusions. Do not argue with Mormons about polygamy, baptism for the dead or temples. Do not argue with the followers of Armstrong as to whether or not we should eat lobster. Do not bother arguing with a Moonie as to whether or not Moon's recent time in jail was valid.

The only issue that must be dealt with when confronted

by a cultist is the issue of religious authority. As long as this cult member is resting on the absolute and infallible authority of the cult leadership, there is nothing you will ever be able to say or show him which will in any way affect him. You can show him Bible verses and give him theological arguments until you are blue in the face and he will ignore everything you say. You must destroy the religious authority of the cult leadership.

The most effective way of dealing with the authority of cultic leaders is to use the principle stated in Deut. 18:21, 22.

> "You may say to yourselves, 'How can we know when a message has not been spoken by the Lord?' If what a prophet proclaims in the name of the Lord does not take place or come true, that is a message the Lord has not spoken. That prophet has spoken presumptuously. Do not be afraid of him."

In the above passage, God's Word tells us that we can identify a false prophet when his predictions concerning the future fail to materialize. You will also notice that it only takes one false prophecy to identify a false prophet. No amount of rationalizing can avoid the inevitable logic of the passage.

> "If someone is God's prophet then his predictions will not fail. If someone's predictions fail then he is not God's prophet."

The denial of the consequence is always valid in logic. This approach immediately cuts through all extraneous issues and goes to the central and foundational problem between the Christian and the cults. The Christian looks to God's Word as being the final authority in all matters of faith, life and practice. The cultist looks to the cult leadership as providing him with his doctrine and guidance. The conflict is irreconcilable.

Summary

Just because someone says that he is a Christian does not mean that he is really a Christian. We must not be so gullible as to accept religious groups on face value. They must define their terms before we can accept them as fellow Christians.

Questions for Discussion

1. What is a cult?
2. How does Deut. 18:21-22 help us refute cult leaders?
3. What are the signs of a cult?
4. What is the key issue when dealing with cultists?
5. If someone says that he believes in Jesus, how are you to respond?
6. You are asked to go to a Bible study on campus. What questions should you ask before you go?
7. A campus group invites you to a free weekend retreat at a ranch; should you go?

TWELVE

Some Popular Cults

Perhaps you are wondering why the subject of the cults or the occult would be included in this manual. The reason is quite simple. As a college student you will be asked to join several different cultic groups during your college career. It does not matter if it happens to be the Moonies or the Hare Krishnas, you will be confronted with cult members who will try to recruit you to their group.

It was for this reason Jesus gave a warning nearly 2000 years ago that His followers must be prepared to encounter religious deception. False christs and false prophets will try to deceive the people of God.

> "Watch out that no one deceives you. Many false prophets will appear and deceive many people. At that time if anyone says to you, 'Look, here is the Christ!'or, 'There he is!' do not believe it. For false Christs and false prophets will appear and perform great signs and miracles to deceive even the elect — if that were possible. See, I have told you ahead of time. So if anyone tells you, 'There he is, out in the desert,' do not go out; or, 'Here he is, in the inner rooms,' do not believe it. For as the lightning comes from the east and flashes to the west, so will be the coming of the Son of Man."
>
> (Matt. 24:4, 23-27)

The following material will introduce you to some of the popular cultic groups and will give you the ammunition you need to deal with them quickly and effectively. Keep to the issue of religious authority. Do not deal with peripheral issues. Deal only with the question: Is this leadership a false prophet or a true prophet?

These brief overviews are not intended to teach the history or theology of the cult in question. We are only seeking to give you a brief answer that can be remembered and utilized easily. For further study consult the bibliography. "Be prepared" should be your motto.

Jehovah's Witnesses

The Jehovah's Witness cult is based upon the religious authority of its leadership who has repeatedly claimed down through the years to be God's prophet on earth and that their doctrines are revealed to them by angels.

In terms of predicting dates, the Watchtower Society has been 100% consistent in that every time they have predicted the future, the prediction failed! They have consistently failed the test of Deut. 18:21, 22.

The Jehovah's Witnesses originally taught that the "last days" began in 1799, Jesus returned invisibly in 1874 and the end of the world would take place in 1914. When 1914 came and went without Armageddon, they reprinted the same books and inserted the date 1915. When 1915 didn't work out, they reprinted the books with 1916 as the new date.

It was in 1916 that their founder, Charles Russell, died and the new president, Rutherford, took over. He immediately pointed to 1918 as the new date for the end of the world. But when 1918 proved to be another false prophecy, he published a book entitled, *Millions Now Living Will Never Die,* in which it was stated that 1925 would be the end of the world.

When 1925 did not materialize as expected, they tried to prop up the hopes of Jehovah's Witnesses by building a mansion in San Diego called Beth Sarim where Abraham, Isaac and Jacob would live after their bodily resurrection perhaps in 1929 or thereafter. Needless to say, they never showed up. So, Rutherford moved into the mansion.

In the 1930's they dropped the 1874 date as the invisible return of Christ and substituted 1914 in its place. Most Jehovah's Witnesses do not know that the Society switched Christ's return from 1874 to 1914.

In recent times, 1975 stands out as the clearest example of the Watchtower's attempt to predict the end of the world. In Watchtower books, magazines and taped sermons, 1975 was predicted to be the end of the world. Jehovah's Witnesses were encouraged to cash in their life insurance policies, sell their homes and quit their jobs in order to be involved in full time work for the Watchtower society.

When 1975 did not see the end of the world, 27% of the Jehovah's Witnesses left the organization. Since that time, Jehovah's Witnesses have now been instructed by the leadership to deny that the Society ever said anything about 1975.

One of the difficulties in dealing with the Jehovah's Witnesses is that in their book, *Aid to Bible Understanding,* the Watchtower defines a lie as not telling the truth to someone who deserves it. Anyone who opposes the Watchtower does not deserve the truth and, hence, may be lied to freely.

This explains why Jehovah's Witnesses who know that 1975 was predicted to be the end of the world, will say that the Watchtower never said anything about the date 1975. They have been told to lie to anyone who brings up all the false prophecies of the Society.

This is where the documents come in handy. Instead of allowing the burden of proof to be upon you, you must place the burden of proof on the Jehovah's Witness to demonstrate that their prophecies came true. If they cannot show how these predictions came true, then the Watchtower is a false prophet. The documents are presented in Robert Morey's *How to Answer a Jehovah's Witness.*

Jehovah's Witnesses have also now been instructed to say

that the Watchtower has never claimed to be a prophet. Ask them to obtain for you a copy of the April 1, 1972 Watchtower magazine in which there is an article entitled "And They Shall Know That a Prophet Was Among Them." In this article, the Watchtower claims to be God's prophet.

Some Jehovah's Witnesses will admit under pressure that the Watchtower has predicted the end of the world many times. But they dismiss this on the grounds that "everyone makes mistakes." Point out to them that while everyone makes mistakes, not everyone claims to be God's prophet on earth! A false prophecy is not the same thing as a mistake. Do you claim that you get your doctrines directly from angels?

If you stick to the issue of the false prophecies of the Watchtower, you will have success in winning Jehovah's Witnesses to Christ. In one survey we took of ex-Jehovah's Witnesses who are now Christians, we found that in the vast majority of cases, they became Christians as a result of seeing that the Watchtower was a false prophet.

Mormons

There are over a dozen different Mormon denominations which all claim to be the "true church." But unless you live in the Midwest, you probably only encounter missionaries of the Church of Jesus Christ of Latter Day Saints (LDS) which has its headquarters in Salt Lake City, Utah.

Regardless if you are dealing with the Latter Day Saints or one of the other Mormon churches, all of them have one thing in common. They all claim that Joseph Smith was God's prophet and that his doctrines are to be received as coming directly from God.

The claims of Smith are so fantastic that there are only three possible logical responses we can have about him.

1. He was a prophet of God.
2. He was crazy.
3. He was a liar.

If he was a prophet of God, then we should all become Mormons. But since there are a dozen competing Mormon denominations all claiming to be the "true" church of Smith, this might be difficult. If he was crazy, he should have been locked up and his followers are to be pitied. If he deceived people in order to obtain money, sex and power, then he should be exposed as a fraud.

How can we know which of these three opinions we should take of Joseph Smith? Deut. 18:21, 22 tells us to test the predictions of Joseph Smith. As a matter of record, Smith gave many prophecies concerning the future. If these prophecies did not come to pass, he was a false prophet.

Even though the prophetic test found in Deut. 18 seems quite reasonable and straightforward, Mormons have been told by their leaders to evade this test. In order to prove that Joseph Smith was a prophet, they are instructed to argue in a circle and base everything on a "burning witness" in the heart.

In their circular argument, Mormons will say, "Joseph Smith was a prophet of God because God spoke to him." But if you ask them how do they know that God spoke to Joseph Smith, they reply, "God spoke to Joseph Smith because he was a prophet of God!"

Just as a dog chasing his tail or someone rowing with only one oar never seems to get anywhere, the circular argument that Joseph Smith was a prophet because God spoke to him and God spoke to him because he was a prophet will never go anywhere either.

Subjective feelings or "a burning witness in the heart" is the next argument that Mormons are encouraged to give. Mormons have memorized and will repeat something like this,

> "I know that Joseph Smith is a prophet of God and the Book of Mormon is the Word of God because I got on my knees and I asked God to give me a burning witness in my heart if these things were so. I now bear you my testimony that I have a burning witness in my heart that Joseph Smith was indeed the prophet of God and the Book of Mormon is the Word of God."

What the Mormon fails to recognize is that the members of any major religious group would state that their "heart" tells them that they are right. But feelings do not prove anything. One way to drive this home is to respond to the Mormon immediately after he has borne his testimony by saying,

"And I bear you my testimony that I have a burning witness in my heart that Joseph Smith was a false prophet and the Book of Mormon is a fraud."

Once you have refuted the Mormon's attempt to use circular reasoning and subjective feelings, you have cleared the way to deal with the prophecies and predictions of Joseph Smith.

Joseph Smith's False Prophecies

Joseph Smith made over sixty false prophecies. The following prophecies are particularly useful in dealing with Mormons. The documentation for these and other false prophecies can be found in Robert Morey's *How to Answer a Mormon.*

1. In 1835, Joseph Smith clearly taught that Jesus Christ would return and the end of the world would happen around 1891 or 1892. That he predicted the end of the world is clear from the documentation found in such church literature as the *History of the Church,* Vol. 2. pg. 182. It is also found in the diaries and sermons which were written during this same time period. For example, in the journal of Oliver Boardman Hamington, vol. 2. pgs. 128-129, we read,

"On the 14th of February, 1835, Joseph Smith said that God had revealed to him the coming of Christ would be within 56 years which being added to 1835 shows that before 1891 and the 14th of February the Savior of the world would make his appearance again upon the earth and the winding up scene take place."

The documentation which reveals that Joseph Smith predicted the end of the world is so clear that Mormons try to "stonewall" the situation. But just keep hammering home the fact that Smith predicted the end of the world and it did not happen. Thus he was a false prophet.

2. Joseph Smith prophesied that people live on the moon who are 6 feet in height, live to be 1000 years old, and dress like Quakers. If there are no 1000 year old, 6 ft. Quakers on the moon, Joseph Smith was not a prophet of God.

Once again, the documentation for the prophecy of Joseph Smith concerning men on the moon is so full and clear that Mormons have to pretend that it does not exist. But in official church literature published during the early history of the Mormon church we find such statements as,

> "As far back as 1837, I know that he [Joseph Smith] said the moon was inhabited by men and women the same as this earth, and that they lived to a greater age than we do — that they live generally to near the age of a 1000 years. He described the men as averaging near 6 ft. in height, and dressing quite uniformly in something near the Quaker style. In my patriarchal blessing, given by the father Joseph the Prophet, in Kirkland, 1837, I was told that I should preach the Gospel before I was eleven years of age and that I should preach the Gospel to the inhabitants upon the islands of the sea, and to the inhabitants of the moon, even the planet you can now behold with your eyes."
> (*Young Woman's Journal,* 1892, pgs. 263-264)

Brigham Young taught that people lived on the sun as well as the moon! In *The Journal of Discourses,* Vol. 13, pg. 271, Young states,

> "Who can tell us of the inhabitants of this little planet that shines of an evening, called the moon? When you inquire about the inhabitants of that sphere you find that the most learned are as ignorant in regard to them as the most ignorant of their fellows. So it is in regard to the inhabitants of the sun. Do you think it is in-

habited? I rather think it is. Do you think there is any life there? No question about it: it was not made in vain.''

Not only did Joseph Smith say that there were 6 ft, 1000 year old Quakers living on the moon, but Brigham Young added that there were people living on the sun!

3. On August 6, 1836, Joseph Smith prophesied that he was going to go to Salem, Massachusetts and that he would return with enough money to pay all the debts of his followers and with a large group of converts.

This prophecy is recorded in the Mormon scriptures such as *Doctrine and Covenants,* chapter 111, verses 2, 4 and 5. This prophecy completely failed. Smith returned with his saddle bags empty and only a small group of converts. It is no wonder that contemporary diaries record Mormons who left the church because they saw that Joseph Smith was a false prophet.

These are some of the clear false prophecies made by Joseph Smith that are recorded in official Mormon literature or in the early writings of the Mormon church. These false prophecies must be taken at face value and evaluated according to Deut. 18:21-22. Even one of the presidents of the Latter Day Saints Church has stated,

"If God has not spoken, if the angel of God has not appeared to Joseph Smith, and if these things are not true of which we speak, then the whole thing is an imposture from beginning to end. There is no halfway house, no middle path about the matter; it is either one thing or the other."

(Journal of Discourses, Vol. 21, pg. 165)

Another Mormon president, Joseph Fielding Smith, added to this,

"Mormonism, as it is called, must stand or fall on the story of Joseph Smith. He was either a prophet of God, divinely called, properly appointed and commissioned,

or he was one of the biggest frauds this world has ever seen. There is no middle ground. If Joseph Smith was a deceiver, who willfully attempted to mislead the people, then he should be exposed; his claim should be refuted, and his doctrine shown to be false."
(*Doctrines of Salvation,* 1959, Vol. 1, pgs. 188-189)

Do not let your Mormon friends off the hook. If there are no 6 ft., 1000 year old Quakers on the moon, if there are no people living on the sun and the end of the world did not take place in 1891, then Joseph Smith was a false prophet.

The Moonies

In dealing with Moonies, always deal with the person of Moon himself. Do not argue over doctrine or politics. Concentrate on the authority of Moon.

The Unification Church is in a unique situation in which the leader, Mr. Moon, is not only a cult leader but also involved in the occult.

As a cultic leader, Moon's authority is above Scripture. He views himself as the "Second Lord of the advent." He claims to be the physical manifestation of the divine principle in human form. Moon's view of God is that of Eastern religions in which "God" is the yin and the yang, the positive and the negative, the male and the female principle of the universe. He views himself as the incarnation of this impersonal principle of opposites and thus as the true representative of God on earth.

His authority over his followers is absolute. He can marry them at will and dictate how many children they are to have. No one can contradict him or do other than what he says.

Moon is also into the occult as well as being an occultic leader. Moon is what is classically known as a "shaman." A shaman is someone who claims that they are able to control the spirit world and the forces of nature.

Moon claims to have been a spiritistic clairvoyant from his

youth. He claims that he can see the spirits of the dead. He even claims that he entered the spirit world and there conquered the spirits of Jesus, Moses and Buddha. He has attended seances with such mediums as Arthur Ford.

In dealing with the Moonies you have two approaches. The first approach is to deal with Moon in terms of Deut. 18:21-22. Has Moon made predictions concerning the future which have failed? Yes, he has.

He originally taught that the Lord of the Second Advent would be revealed in 1967. When this prophecy failed, 1980 through '81 or possibly '82 was picked as the time when the world would recognize him and his kingdom would begin. These prophecies obviously failed. He felt that he would receive not only worldwide recognition but acceptance.

In the midst of the Watergate scandal when the resignation of Richard Nixon was being called for, Moon prophesied that "God has chosen Richard Nixon to be President" (*San Francisco Chronicle,* January 19, 1974).

When confronted later with the fact that Nixon resigned, Moon prophesied that Nixon resigned because Communists had threatened to kill him if he did not resign,

> "I am sure there is a Communistic power working behind the scenes. They came to threaten to kill him if he did not resign, and that's what compelled him to do so."
> (*San Francisco Chronicle,* December 10, 1975)

The second approach to dealing with Moonies is to point them to Deut. 18:9-12 where the Bible condemns all attempts to communicate with the dead. Thus seances and mediums in which you try to contact the spirits of the dead are condemned as "abomination unto the Lord." This is what sorcery and witchcraft are all about.

Moon claims in his book, *The Divine Principle,* that he is in communication with the spirits of the dead. Not only did he teach that he was a medium and involved in mediumistic activities, but in his autobiography Arthur Ford reveals that

Moon had a seance with him in which Moon sought to speak to the spirits of the dead. Moon wanted the spirit world to acknowledge him as Lord but they refused. Moon left quite disappointed.

The cultic and occultic activities and teachings of Mr. Moon forever disqualify him from being Lord of anything. He is not the successor to Jesus Christ or Moses for both of them were against sorcery and witchcraft.

One thing you will have to watch out for with the Moonies is their program of "heavenly deception" which involves their lying to get your money or to get you to an isolated spot where they can try to brainwash you. Moonies have been known to ask for donations for drug abuse programs, Christian youth groups, the homeless, the United Way, missions, churches and handicap programs while the money actually goes to uphold Moon's lavish lifestyle.

They will advertise free weekend seminars on pollution, international relations, anti-communist programs, and science. But when you get there, all they want to talk about is Moon! So, don't accept any "free" weekend seminars unless your pastor knows the group.

Seventh Day Adventists

The Seventh Day Adventist Church relies upon the authority of Ellen G. White, whom they view as God's prophet.

> "Seventh Day Adventists hold that Ellen G. White performed the work of a true prophet during the 70 years of her public ministry. As Samuel was a prophet, as Jeremiah was a prophet, as John the Baptist, so we believe that Mrs. White was a prophet to the church of Christ today."
>
> (*The Advent Review and Herald,* 10-4-1928)

Ellen G. White viewed her writings as being as inspired as the writings of the apostle Paul or any other author of Scripture (*E.G. White Testimony,* Vol. 3, pg. 275; Vol. 5, pg. 661). She stated on one occasion,

> "God was speaking through clay. In these letters which I write, in the testimonies I bear, I am presenting to you that which the Lord has presented to me. I do not write one article in the paper expressing merely my own ideas. They are what God has opened before in vision — the precious rays of light shining from the throne."
> (*Visions of Mrs. E.G. White Testimony,* #31, pg. 63)

Just as we applied the test of prophecy to Charles Russell, The Watchtower, Joseph Smith and Moon, we must apply the same test to Ellen G. White. What does the record reveal?

Ellen G. White prophesied that Jesus Christ would return in 1843. She learned this date from William Miller and fully accepted it as valid (*Early Writings,* pg 64, 1882 edition). She even stated in 1844,

> "We heard the voice of God like many waters, which gave us the day and hour of Jesus' coming."
> (*A Word to the Little Flock,* pg. 14, 1847 edition)

When the 1843 date failed, she tried 1844. When that date failed to materialize she said confidently in 1845,

> "It is well known that many were expecting the Lord to come at the 7th month, 1845, that Christ would then come we firmly believed. A few days before the time passed . . . Ellen was with one of the band at Carver, Mass., where she saw in a vision, that we should be disappointed."
> (*A Word to the Little Flock,* pg. 22, 1847 edition)

In 1849, she taught that

> "the time is almost finished, and what we have been 6 years learning they will have to learn in months."
> (*Early Writings,* pg. 57)

She was so confident that the Lord was going to return when she predicted that she stated to a group assembled to hear her,

> "I was shown the company present at the conference. Said the angel: Some food for worms, some subjects of the seven last plagues, some will be alive and remain upon the earth to be translated at the coming of Jesus."
> (*Testimonies for the Church,* Vol. 1, pg. 131-132)

The record of those present at this prophecy conference has been discovered and it is clear that all of them have since died.

The evidence has also revealed that she was a lying prophet in that she plagiarized her books from the works of others. See Walter Rea's book, *The White Lie.* This includes her so-called "visions of health" as well as her Bible studies. See Ronald Numbers' book, *Prophetess of Health.* She was dishonest when she put her name on other people's writings and claimed that they had come to her in a vision from God.

Summary

The Christian must be alert to those cults which prey on college students. Do not be intimidated by them but witness to them of the saving grace of God and the freedom you have found in Christ.

Questions for Discussion

1. Did the Jehovah's Witnesses ever predict the end of the world?
2. How do Mormons use circular reasoning?
3. Can a subjective feeling prove anything?

4. What evidence is there to show that Joseph Smith was not a prophet of God?
5. What can you say to a Moonie?
6. What claims did Mrs. White make? Was she a true or false prophet?
7. Did she copy her books from the works of others?
8. Where did she get her "visions" of health?

T H I R T E E N

The Occult and Parapsychology

T he occult has to do with those rites, ideas, practices and miraculous feats connected with witchcraft. The word "occult" itself means hidden or unseen because it was used to refer to those satanic rites which were forbidden by law during the Middle Ages. Those who desired to practice witchcraft had to do so while hidden or unseen in order to escape civil prosecution.

Its Recent History

At the beginning of the 19th century, the occult was renamed as "spiritualism" or "spiritism." Later Theosophy renamed it "psychic forces" or "psychic power."

With the beginning of the Society of Psychical Research (SPR), witchcraft and sorcery were proclaimed as being scientifically neutral and representing the "natural" mental abilities of man.

When the theory of evolution became popular the idea arose that perhaps the human race was evolving in terms of psychic powers so that what formerly was done only by a witch or sorcerer could now be done by everyone.

It was J.B. Rhine in the 1950's who made "psychic power" a subject of valid research in the scientific community. He was the one who invented the term Extra-Sensory Perception or

E.S.P. What was formerly known as sorcery was now labeled as E.S.P.

Rhine had been introduced to the occult through Arthur Conan Doyle who was one of the most dynamic representatives of the Society of Psychical Research. It was Rhine's hope to demonstrate scientifically that what was formerly understood to be satanic or witchcraft was only man's natural psychic powers.

Today witchcraft and sorcery are called "parapsychology." But we must remember that a rose called by any other name smells the same. What the Bible condemns as witchcraft and sorcery is nothing more than what is called E.S.P. or parapsychology today.

While modern humanists are willing to view such things as bending spoons or levitating objects as being representative of "psychic forces," the Christian knows that this is simply the same old occult that has plagued the world since man's fall into sin. For a detailed history of the occult, see Robert Morey's *Death and the Afterlife.*

Why People Get Into the Occult

Why do people become involved in the occult? Some people become involved in the occult because they want to communicate with dead loved ones. Perhaps a favorite aunt or uncle has died and they wish to contact them. Or their husband or child has died and they feel lonely without them.

Secondly, some people become involved because they want to know the future. They want to know if they will marry or have children in the future. They want to know the stock market or what the commodities market will yet bring.

Thirdly, some people go into the occult because they want power. They want the power to heal themselves, to cast spells on other people or to get rich. Of course, they must pay with their immortal soul to get it.

Fourthly, some people want to contact Satan or the

demonic host through the occultic rite. They desire to be in his service and will do acts of blasphemy and sign contracts in their own blood in which they sell their soul to Satan. Satanism is widespread today and is growing at a dangerous rate.

Fifthly, some people get involved with the occult simply to satisfy their curiosity or their need for excitement. When they play with the Ouija board or go to a seance, this gives them a thrill because it is a frightening experience. But what they do not understand is that playing with the occult is like juggling nitroglycerin. They just might destroy themselves.

The Origin of the Occult

Where does the occult derive its power? God has never been interested in doing parlor tricks in order to amuse people. He does not have the slightest interest in making tables dance or bugles float in the air. He will not make a spoon bend in order to entertain an audience. When Jesus was asked to perform miracles to entertain King Herod, He refused (Lk. 23:8-12).

Neither Jesus nor the Apostles viewed the miracles they did as coming from some kind of "inner psychic force" (see: John 5:19; Acts 3:12-13). Even the Old Testament prophets acknowledged that the miracles they did came from God and not from their own power (Gen. 41:16). This refutes modern parapsychologists who claim that the miracles of the Bible were simply the results of natural human powers.

On the other hand, the authors of Scriptures clearly indicate that they viewed all supernatural feats that did not come from God as coming from Satan himself (Acts 16:16-18). Those who were controlled by demonic forces could do miraculous feats (Matt. 24:24).

This was the perspective of Scripture because Satan has always tried to counterfeit God's miracles by producing his own miracles (Matt. 24:24; II Thessalonians 2:9; Revelation 13:11-17). The magicians of Pharaoh sought to match Moses miracle for miracle (Exo. 7-9).

The Important Thing to Remember

The important thing to remember is that just because something is real does not mean that it is good. Just because some supernatural event took place does not mean that God is behind it.

Some people are so foolish as to believe such statements as, "All healing comes from God" or "All miracles come from God." There is another power or force in this universe of which the Bible speaks. This power is evil and very dangerous.

We must also remember whatever diseases or sicknesses Satan has inflicted on someone, he can readily remove. This is the kind of counterfeit miracle Satan does. Just because something is a miracle or a demonstration of power, does not mean that God did it. Be not deceived.

All occult practices are condemned in Scriptures as being satanic in origin and power (Deut. 18). Thus they are an abomination to God and forbidden to His people.

The Christian must also be prepared for much fraud in this area. A competent magician or illusionist can reproduce most of the so-called "miracles" or "psychic" feats of those who claim paranormal abilities. They can bend spoons by trickery and make objects appear to float around in mid-air. There are even Christian illusionists who have debunked well known religious con artists who were duping people with common magician's tricks.

Summary

Christians should not engage in any parapsychological experiments to develop their E.S.P. powers. As a matter of fact, they do not need E.S.P. because they have H.S.P. (Holy Spirit Power)!

The Christian does not fear Satan for "Greater is He that is in us than he that is in the world" (I John 4:4). God's truth and God's kingdom will ultimately triumph over the kingdom and lies of the devil. Don't become entangled in the forces of darkness under the guise of the ''science'' of parapsychology.

Questions for Discussion

1. What is the occult and how does it relate to modern parapsychology?
2. If a psychic feat is not a fraud, where did its power come from?
3. Should Christians live in fear of the devil?
4. Who invented E.S.P.?
5. Did the prophets, apostles or Jesus use E.S.P. to do their miracles?
6. Should Christians get involved in parapsychological experiments?
7. What does Deut. 18 say about the occult?
8. What important point should be remembered?

Conclusion

T he Christian student today has a great opportunity to influence his generation for Christ. As we approach the
21st Century, the Gospel is fast becoming the "only game
in town" that offers hope to a lost humanity. The secular
world views have nothing to offer people. All they can do
is to deny the existence of God, the inspiration of the Bible,
the historicity of Christ, and the Christian values and morals on which Western civilization depends. Their anti-
morality "free-sex" crusade has resulted in a plague of
V.D., AIDS, teen pregnancies, abortion, child molesting and
rape.

Now is the time for Christian students to take over their
campus for Christ. As soldiers of Jesus Christ they must
be tough-minded. They must throw off any feelings of inferiority. After all, they have the truth, the whole truth and
nothing but the truth! Why should they be intimidated by
the humanists, cultists and pagans on campus?

They need to stand up and speak out for the cause of
God and truth. They must not allow the anti-Christian
forces to deny their civil rights to say what they believe.
The pagans do not hesitate to say what they believe. Christians have just as much a right to defend Christianity just
as pagans have to knock it.

If millions of Christian students would get on fire for
Jesus Christ, God would send us a new Reformation in

which millions of people will come to know the Lord Jesus Christ and Western culture would be reclaimed for Christ. It can be done if we are willing to obey God's Word.

Bibliography

C hristian students should possess and read the following books in order to be prepared to defend their faith while at college. The books are arranged topically.

I. Answers for atheists, agnostics and skeptics:

C.S. Lewis, *Mere Christianity* (MacMillan, N.Y., 1960)

C.S. Lewis, *Miracles* (MacMillan, N.Y., 1966)

J. Edwin Orr, *Faith That Makes Sense* (Judson Press, Valley Forge, 1965)

Gordon H. Clark, *A Christian View of Men and Things* (The Trinity Foundation, Jefferson, Maryland, 1988)

Gordon H. Clark, *God's Hammer:The Bible and Its Critics* (The Trinity Foundation, Jefferson Foundation, 1987)

Gordon H. Clark, *Religion, Reason and Revelation* (The Trinity Foundation, Jefferson Foundation, 1986)

John Warwick Montgomery, *Christianity for the Tough Minded* (Bethany House, Minn., 1973)

John Warwick Montgomery, *History & Christianity* (InterVarsity Press, Downers Grove, 1979)

John Warwick Montgomery, *Where Is History Going?* (Bethany House, Minn., 1969)

Robert A. Morey, *The New Atheism and the Erosion of Freedom* (Crowne Publications, P.O. Box 688, Southbridge, Ma. 01550, 1989)

Robert A. Morey, *A Christian Handbook for Defending the Faith* (Crowne Publications, P.O. Box 688, Southbridge, Ma. 01550, 1989)

Francis A. Schaeffer, *Back to Freedom and Dignity* (InterVarsity Press, 1972)

Francis A. Schaeffer, *Escape From Reason* (InterVarsity Press, Downers Grove, 1969)

Francis A. Schaeffer, *He Is There and Is Not Silent* (InterVarsity Press, Downers Grove, 1972)

Francis A. Schaeffer, *How Should We Then Live?* (Fleming Revell, Old Tappan, 1976)

Francis A. Schaeffer, *The God Who Is There* (InterVarsity Press, Downers Grove, 1968)

Josh McDowell, *Evidence That Demands a Verdict* (Campus Crusade for Christ, Arrowhead Springs, 1972)

Josh McDowell, *More Evidence That Demands a Verdict* (Campus Crusade for Christ, Arrowhead Springs, 1975)

Josh McDowell & Don Stewart, *Understanding Secular Religions* (Campus Crusade for Christ, Arrowhead Springs, 1982)

II. Answers for those who deny that Jesus ever existed:

Norman Anderson, *Jesus Christ: The Witness of History* (InterVarsity Press, Downers Grove, 1985)

F. F. Bruce, *Jesus & Christian Origins Outside the New Testament* (Eerdmans, Grand Rapids, 1974)

E. M. Blaiklock, *Jesus Christ: Man or Myth?* (Thomas Nelson, Nashville, 1984)

Gary R. Habermas, *Ancient Evidence for the Life of Jesus* (Thomas Nelson, Nashville, 1984)

Robert A. Morey, *The New Atheism and the Erosion of Freedom* (Crowne Publications, P.O. Box 688, Southbridge, Ma. 01550, 1989)

Edwin M. Yamauchi, *Pre-Christian Gnosticism* (Baker, Grand Rapids, 1983)

III. The Christian world view:

Robert A. Morey, *A Christian Handbook for Defending the Faith* (Crowne Publications, P.O. Box 688, Southbridge, Ma., 01550, 1989)

Francis A. Schaeffer, *Genesis in Space and Time* (InterVarsity Press, Downers Grove, 1972)

IV. Christians in politics:

Francis Schaeffer, *A Christian Manifesto* (Crossway, Westchester, 1981)

V. The problem of pollution:

Francis A. Schaeffer, *Pollution and the Death of Man* (Tyndale, Wheaton, 1970)

VI. Abortion, infanticide, mercy killing and euthanasia:

Francis A. Schaeffer, *Whatever Happened to the Human Race?* (Fleming Revell, Old Tappan, 1979)

VII. A Christian response to drug abuse:

Robert A. Morey, *How to Keep Your Kids Drug-free* (Crowne Publications, P.O. Box 688, Southbridge, Ma., 01550, 1989)

VIII. Christian view of war:

Robert A. Morey, *When Is It Right to Fight?* (Bethany House, Minn., 1985)

IX. Christian view of ethics:

Norman L. Geisler, *Ethics: Alternatives and Issues* (Zondervan, Grand Rapids, 1979)

Erwin Lutzer, *The Necessity of Ethical Absolutes* (Zondervan, Grand Rapids, 1981)

Robert A. Morey, *A Christian Handbook for Defending the Faith* (Crowne Publications, P.O. Box 688, Southbridge, Ma., 01550, 1989)

X. Science:

Gordon H. Clark, *The Philosophy of Science and Belief in God* (The Trinity Foundation, Jefferson, Maryland, 1987)

XI. Death and the immortality of the soul:

Robert A. Morey, *Death and the Afterlife* (Bethany House, Minn., 1984)

XII. The cults and the occult:

Walter R. Martin, *The Kingdom of the Cults* (Bethany House, Minn., 1977)

Walter R. Martin, *The New Cults* (Vision House, Ventura, 1984)

Robert A. Morey, *Horoscopes and the Christian* (Bethany House, Minn., 1981)

Robert A. Morey, *Reincarnation and Christianity* (Bethany House, Minn., 1980)

Robert A. Morey, *How to Answer a Jehovah's Witness* (Bethany House, Minn., 1982)

Robert A. Morey, *How to Answer a Mormon* (Bethany House, Minn., 1983)

David Hunt & T. A. McMahon, *The Seduction of Christianity* (Harvest House, Eugene, Or., 1985)

Wilson & Weldon, *Occult Shock & Psychic Forces* (Master Books, San Diego, 1980)

XIII. Eastern religions:

Pat Means, *The Mystical Maze* (Campus Crusade for Christ, Arrowhead Springs, 1976)

Rabindranath R. Maharaj, *Death of a Guru* (Holman, N.Y., 1977)

Lit sen Chang, *Zen-Existentialism* (Pres. & Ref., Harmony, 1969)

XIV. The Christian concept of God:
Robert A. Morey, *Battle of the Gods* (Crowne Publications, P.O. Box 688, Southbridge, Ma. 01550, 1989)

XV. Christian view of art:
H. R. Rookmaaker, *Modern Art and the Death of a Culture* (InterVarsity Press, Downers Grove, 1975)

Francis A. Schaeffer, *Art and the Bible* (InterVarsity Press, Downers Grove, 1974)

Robert A. Morey, *A Christian Handbook for Defending the Faith* (Crowne Publications, P.O. Box 688, Southbridge, Ma. 01550, 1989)

XVI. The New Age Movement:
Constance Cumbey, *The Hidden Dangers of the Rainbow* (Huntington House, Shreveport, 1983)

Walter R. Martin, *The New Age Cult* (Bethany House, Minn., 1988)

Douglas R. Groothuis, *Unmasking the New Age* (InterVarsity Press, Downers Grove, 1986)

XVII. Answers for alleged contradictions in the Bible:
Gleason Archer, *Encyclopedia of Bible Difficulties* (Zondervan, Grand Rapids,1982)

XVIII. What the founding fathers believed:
Timothy LaHaye, *Faith of Our Founding Fathers* (Woglemuth & Hyatt, Brentwood, Tn., 1988)

XIX. The atonement:
Robert A. Morey, *The Saving Work of Christ* (Crowne Publications, P.O. Box 688, Southbridge, Ma. 01550, 1989)

XX. The biblical concept of worship:
Robert A. Morey, *Worship Is All of Life* (Crowne Publications, P.O. Box 688, Southbridge, Ma. 01550, 1989)

XXI. Christian discipleship:
Robert A. Morey, *A Discipleship Manual for Christians* (Crowne Publications, P.O. Box 688, Southbridge, Ma. 01550, 1989, vols. I & II)